實用

中國菜
CHINESE
COOKING
FOR BEGINNERS

編著
黃淑惠

烹飪製作
李木村、葉佳祖

文稿協助
林淑華、殷宗寧

翻譯
賴燕貞

攝影
大野現

封面設計
曲靜

內頁設計
王瑾、張方馨

印刷
中華彩色印刷股份有限公司

版權所有
局版台業字第0179號

1981年5月初版　35-42-5
2006年9月修訂7版　7-6-0

Author
Huang Su-Huei

Food Presentation
Mu-Tsun Lee
Jia-Tzu Yeh

Editorial Staff
Sophia Lin, John Holt

Translation
Yen-Jen Lai

Photography
Aki Ohno

Cover Design
Jean Chu

Book Design
Chin Ong, F. Chang

Wei-Chuan Publishing
1455 Monterey Pass Rd.,
Suite 110,
Monterey Park, CA 91754,
U.S.A.

Tel: 323-261-3880
Fax: 323-261-3299
wc@weichuancookbook.com
www.weichuancookbook.com

First Printing
May 1981

Revised Edition
1st Printing: October 1994
7th Printing: October 2006

ISBN-13: 978-0-941676-30-4
ISBN-10: 0-941676-30-7
(English/Chinese)

ISBN 0-941676-33-1
(English/Spanish)

ISBN 0-941676-34-X
(French/Chinese)

ISBN 0-941676-37-4
(German/Chinese)

Printed in Taiwan

Contents

目　　錄

Special Ingredients and Sauces
特殊材料

1 **Hoisin Sauce** is made from flour, soy bean, sugar and other fragrant spices. It is sweet and dark.

2 **Fermented Black Beans** are made by cooking, fermenting and then marinating black beans in salt water. The beans are black and taste salty.

3 **Star Anise** (left side) is a fragrant spice used often in Chinese cooking. **Szechuan Peppercorn** (right side) is a spice often used in preparing Szechuan-style dishes.

4 **Oyster Sauce** is made by mixing fermented oysters with water and salt. It has a special seafood flavor.

5 **Sesame Oil** (large bottle) is made by baking or steaming white or black sesame seeds and then extracting the oil. High quality sesame oil has a light color and strong aroma.

6 **Barbecue (Sa Tsa) Sauce** is made by grinding several different kinds of hot and fragrant spices and mixing them together. Ready-made Sa Tsa sauce is also available in markets.

7 **Chinese Black Mushrooms** (right side) are edible fungi that grow on dead tree trunks. Soak them in warm water until soft; cut off stem before using them.
Dried Wood Ears (lower left) are edible fungi that grow on dead tree trunks. The shape resembles a human ear. Soak wood ears in water until soft before using them. Small hard stem should be removed from large wood ears.

1 海鮮醬　麵粉、黃豆、糖及其他辛香料製成的甜味深色醬。

2 豆　豉　將烏豆蒸熟再經醱酵加鹽水釀製，色黑味鹹甘。

3 八　角　（圖左）形似六～八角星型而名之，又稱大茴香。
　花　椒　（圖右）又名山椒或川椒。與八角同為中國菜常用香料。

4 蠔　油　生蠔醱酵加鹽水調製而成，有特殊海鮮美味。

5 麻　油　（圖上）用白或黑芝麻經烤或蒸後榨油製成，高級品色淡味香醇。

6 沙茶醬　各種辛香料磨碎調製而成，味香醇稍辣。

7 香　菇　（圖上）栽培在木頭上的菇類。使用時用溫水泡軟洗淨。
　木　耳　（圖下）生長在朽木上的菌類，因其形狀類似耳朵故稱木耳，使用時用水泡軟洗淨。

Culinary Idioms
烹飪須知

In selecting a menu, consider diversity and quantity of ingredients (balance meat or seafood and vegetables), a combination of color, taste and texture; one dish/person, two dishes/two people, three dishes/three people. Below are recommended techniques which will make your Chinese cooking easier.

菜單的擬定可以一人一菜、二人二菜、三人三菜來考慮，菜式的選擇則以做法難易及材料有葷有素的原則來搭配，以下的要點可幫助讀者掌握烹調技巧。

Measurements
量器容量說明

1 lb. = 16 oz. = 450 g   1 oz. = 28 g   1磅＝16盎司＝450公克   1盎司＝28公克

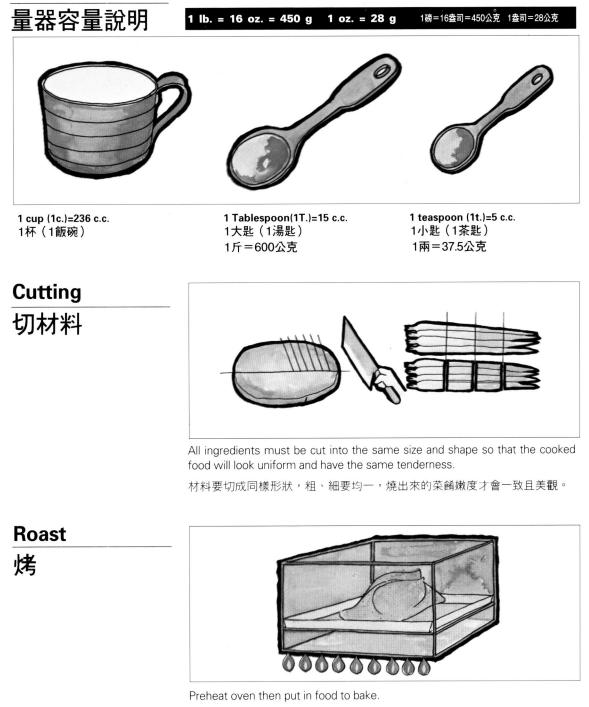

1 cup (1c.)=236 c.c.
1杯（1飯碗）

1 Tablespoon(1T.)=15 c.c.
1大匙（1湯匙）
1斤＝600公克

1 teaspoon (1t.) =5 c.c.
1小匙（1茶匙）
1兩＝37.5公克

Cutting
切材料

All ingredients must be cut into the same size and shape so that the cooked food will look uniform and have the same tenderness.

材料要切成同樣形狀，粗、細要均一，燒出來的菜餚嫩度才會一致且美觀。

Roast
烤

Preheat oven then put in food to bake.

先將烤箱燒熱，再把食物放入烤。

Deep-frying
炸

1 Marinate then coat the food with batter.
先將材料調上味，並視其種類裹上麵糊。

2 Immerse food in heated oil. For foods which take longer to cook, first fry in high heat until the surface is slightly cripsy, then use medium heat and gently stir food to maintainan even temperature. When food is nearly tender, turn heat to high to release oil in food. Remove when done.
炸時先將油燒熱，油份量以略浸食物爲準，不易熟者先將表面炸略乾，無粘狀再以中火炸，並用鍋鏟慢慢推動食物，保持溫度均一，待食物快炸熟前開大火把食物內的油份炸出，食時才不覺油膩。

Stir-frying
炒

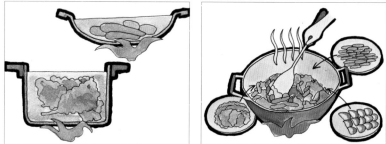

1 Marinate chicken, pork, beef, or fish before stir-frying. Add in cornstarch (and egg white if desired) to tenderize meat. Stir-frying is a quick process. Seasoning sauces and ingredients may be mixed in advance to save cooking time.
炒鷄、豬、牛、魚、蝦等要事先調味，並加太白粉（也可加蛋白），以增加其香嫩。炒菜是速成之菜，炒前若先將佐料分別調在碗內，炒時可節省時間。

2 When several ingredients are used, the difference in tenderness will sometimes require some ingredients to be cooked in oil, boiled, or fried before mixing. When boiling green vegetables, add a little salt and oil. Remove and rinse immediately to keep the color green.
炒菜時因其各材料性質不同，有些須經煮熟後再使用。若需先煮熟靑菜，可在水內加少許鹽及油，撈出後立即沖涼以保顏色靑綠。

3 Stir-frying requires high heat. Heat wok then add oil. Stir-fry green onions, ginger root and garlic until fragrant. Add all other ingredients and seasoning sauce, mix well. Non-stick pan or flat pan may be used for stir-frying.
炒菜時應用大火，首先將鍋燒熱，入油燒熱後，再炒肉類，可免粘鍋；若使用不黏鍋（平底鍋也可）效果良好。

Mix-boil
溜、燴

Boil seasoning sauce or liquid in pan. Add in stir-fried, fried, or cooked food. Thicken with mixture of cornstarch and water.

調味湯汁注入鍋中燒開，隨即加入經過炒、炸或煮熟之食物，再用太白粉及水勾成濃狀。

Steaming
蒸

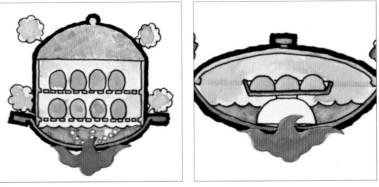

1 Bring water to boil. Place food in a steamer and steam.

將水燒開，再把食物放入蒸籠內藉水蒸氣的熱力把食物蒸熟。

2 **ALTERNATE METHOD:** Place a bowl, upside down on bottom of wok or large pot; add water (do not cover bowl). Put food on a heatproof plate then put plate on the bowl, cover and steam.

簡便蒸法：在鍋底倒扣一只碗加入水至半腰（水量不宜過多以免燒開時觸及食物），上置蒸盤蓋鍋即可蒸。

Stewing
燉

Put water in a large pot. Put ingredients and water or stock, to cover, in a smaller pot and set it inside the large pot. Cook over low heat until food is tender. Soup prepared this way is very light and clear.

所謂燉與蒸略同，外鍋內放水，內鍋放入食物及水或湯（注滿過食物）用慢火經過長時間燉至食物熟軟，做出來的湯汁非常澄清。

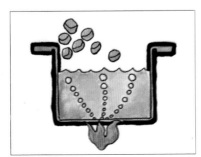

Stock
高湯

Put water in pot; add pork, beef, or chicken meat or bones. Bring to boil and remove scum. Add cooking wine and cook over medium heat for one hour. Remove meat or bones. Stock is ready for use.

用豬、牛、雞的肉或骨頭加入水燒開去除污沫及油漬再加少許酒，以中火煮約1小時，去除肉或骨頭即成高湯。

Assorted Appetizer Plate
serves 12

ABALONE: Use canned abalone meat

BEEF SHANK: See p. 19

HAM: Use cooked ham

SLICED PORK & GARLIC TOPPING: See p. 15

CHINESE ROAST PORK: See p. 11

CRISPY FRIED WALNUTS: See p. 17

SALTED SHRIMP: Clean shrimp; place in salted boiling water; add a little wine and cook 1 minute.

大拼盤
12人份

鮑魚：罐頭鮑魚
五香牛肉：參照第19頁
火腿：洋火腿
白切肉：參照第15頁
叉燒肉：參照第11頁
糖酥核桃：參照第17頁
_, 加小許酒煮

Crispy Salad with Chicken

鷄絲沙拉

1 lb (450g) chicken legs
4 c. shredded lettuce
1 ¹/₂ c. shredded green
   pepper, onion and sliced
   tomato

1 T. ea: soy sauce, vinegar
³/₄ t. ea: sugar, sesame oil
¹/₈ t. salt
dash of pepper
2 T. olive oil

8 won ton skins
oil for deep-frying

1 Boil chicken; when cooked, let cool, bone and shred. Mix **1**, put aside. Cut won ton skins in 1/4" (.5cm) strips, and deep-fry until crispy. Mix all ingredients; serve. May add roasted ground peanuts, sesame seeds and coriander.

☐ **TO DEEP-FRY WON TON SKINS:** Heat oil for deep-frying. Put a strip of won ton in oil. If it stays at the bottom, oil is not hot enough. Allow more time to heat oil. Repeat test. The strip will quickly surface if oil is hot enough. Deep-fry all won ton strips; stir and remove. If oil is too hot, strips will burn.

鷄腿 ……………………12兩
生菜切絲6兩 ……………4杯
青椒、洋蔥（切絲）
　番茄（切片） ………共1¹/₂杯

醋、醬油 …………………各1大匙
糖、麻油 ………………各³/₄小匙
鹽 …………………………¹/₈小匙
胡椒 …………………………少許
沙拉油 ……………………2大匙

餛飩皮 ……………………8張
「炸油」 ……………………適量

1 鷄腿煮熟待冷，去骨，撕成絲或切粗條；將 **1** 料調勻備用。餛飩皮切0.5公分寬條炸酥，食時將全部材料拌勻，可隨喜好加碎花生、芝麻、香菜等。

☐ **炸餛飩皮**：將「炸油」燒熱，先取數條餛飩皮放入油內，如沈底，即表示油溫度太低；如迅速浮起，即可把全部餛飩皮放入炸，並迅速攪動撈起，注意溫度太高則炸出來的餛飩皮焦黑。

Chinese Roast Pork

叉燒肉

2 lbs (900g) shoulder pork

3 T. sugar, 1 ¹/₂ T. soy sauce
1 ¹/₂ T. cooking wine
1 ¹/₂ T. hoisin sauce, 2 t. salt

2 T. soy sauce
hot bean paste, coriander,
   garlic as desired

前腿肉 …………………1斤半

糖 …………………………3大匙
酒、醬油、海鮮醬 ……各1¹/₂大匙
鹽 …………………………2小匙

醬油 ………………………2大匙
辣椒醬、蒜末、香菜 ………隨意

1 **FIRST METHOD:** Cut pork into strips 1 1/2" (4cm) wide; add **1** and marinate overnight. Preheat oven to 400°F (205°C). Put meat on a roasting pan and roast on oven's middle rack 40 minutes; remove, slice and serve with **2**.

2 **SECOND METHOD:** Preheat oven to 400°F (205°C). Cut meat into slices 1/3" (1cm) thick (Fig. 1). Add **1**, marinate as above. Begin at the long edge, roll the meat (Fig. 2) and tie with string (Fig. 3). Roast for 1 hour; remove. Slice and serve with **2**.

1 **條狀形**：肉切4公分寬之長條，調入 **1** 料醃數小時或醃隔夜；烤箱燒熱，將醃好的肉入烤盤置烤箱中層，以400°F烤40分鐘，取出切片沾 **2** 料食之。

2 **捲筒形**：將肉切1公分之厚片（圖1），調入 **1** 料醃數小時或醃隔夜後，捲成筒狀（圖2），用繩扎緊（圖3），烤約60分鐘，取出切片沾 **2** 料食之。

Fig. 1

Fig. 2

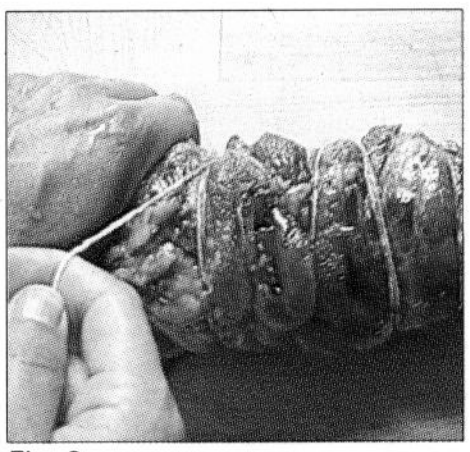

Fig. 3

Crispy-Skin Duck

脆皮鴨

1 duck, 4 lbs (1800g)

1 green onion
2 slices ginger root
½ T. ea: salt, cooking wine
½ t. five-spice powder or
pepper

10 c. water
3 T. salt

1 ½ T. honey

hoisin sauce or sour plum
sauce as desired*

鴨1隻 ··························3斤
蔥 ···························1枝
薑 ···························2片
酒、鹽 ···················各½大匙
五香粉或胡椒 ···············½小匙

水 ··························10杯
鹽 ·························3大匙

蜂蜜 ·····················1½大匙

海鮮醬或酸梅醬* ··············適量

1 Clean duck, drain water from cavity and pat dry. Rub cavity with **1** ; close cavity (Fig. 1).

2 Bring **2** to boil and ladle over entire surface of duck several times (Fig. 2). Spread honey on surface of duck (Fig. 3). Place (hang) duck in a well ventilated place or in refrigerator at least 24 hours. The drier the skin, the crispier it will be after roasting.

3 Pre-heat oven to 400°F (205°C). Place duck on baking pan then roast on oven's middle rack until color is golden; reduce heat to 350°F (178°C) and roast 1 more hour. Serve with **3**.

* Sour plum sauce: Cook 4 T. ea sugar and water, 2 crushed sour plums (seeds removed) and 1/2 T. ketchup for 5 minutes or until thick. Hot chili paste may be added as desired.

1 鴨洗淨拭乾肚內水份，將拌勻的 **1** 料在鴨肚內抹勻，開口處縫合（圖1）。

2 將 **2** 料燒滾多次，澆淋在鴨上（圖2），塗抹蜂蜜於鴨皮（圖3），吊在通風處（或冰箱內）吹乾24小時以上。鴨皮吹得愈乾，烤出的鴨皮愈脆。

3 烤箱燒熱至400℉，鴨盛入烤盤，置烤箱中層，將鴨兩面烤至上色，再用350℉將鴨烤60分鐘至熟，沾 **3** 料食用。

* 酸梅醬：將糖、水各4大匙，酸梅2粒（去籽壓碎），番茄醬½大匙，燒煮5分鐘至汁呈濃稠狀，可隨意加入辣椒醬即成。

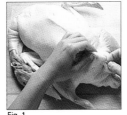
Fig. 1

Fig. 2

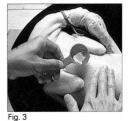
Fig. 3

Jellyfish Salad

拌蜇皮

1/2 lb (225g) salted jellyfish

2/3 T. ea: soy sauce, vinegar
2/3 T. sesame oil
1/2 t. sugar

海蜇皮 ⋯⋯⋯⋯⋯⋯⋯⋯⋯6兩

醬油、醋、麻油 ⋯⋯⋯ 各 $\frac{2}{3}$ 大匙
糖 ⋯⋯⋯⋯⋯⋯⋯⋯⋯ $\frac{1}{2}$ 小匙

1 Use thick, golden jellyfish (Fig. 1). Shred jellyfish into thin strips, wash and drain. Bring 2 C. water to boil; turn off heat. Plunge jellyfish into the water and stir quickly, until curled, immediately remove (Fig. 2). Plunge jellyfish into cold water and rinse several times until cold. Soak jellyfish 8 hours, changing water frequently, until slightly larger and crunchy (Fig. 3). Drain jellyfish, mix with **1**. May be served as an appetizer.

☐ Marinate 1/3 lb (150g) shredded cucumber or white radish in 1/2 t. salt for 1 hour; rinse and squeeze to dry. Mix cucumber with 1 t. each, vinegar and sugar. The prepared cucumber may be tossed with jellyfish and served.

1 海蜇皮選厚、金黃色為佳（圖1），切0.5公分寬之長條，洗淨瀝乾；水2杯燒開即熄火，隨入蜇皮絲，迅速拌開見捲起即撈出（圖2），用水漂洗數次至冷卻，再加水浸泡8小時，需時時換水，泡至蜇皮漲開伸直即可（圖3），瀝乾並調入 **1** 料拌勻食用。此菜餚適合當前菜。

☐ 將黃瓜或白蘿蔔絲4兩，用鹽 $\frac{1}{2}$ 小匙醃1小時洗淨瀝乾，拌入醋、糖各1小匙，可與蜇皮絲拌食。

Sliced Pork & Garlic Topping

白切肉

1 lb (450g) pork shoulder
  roast

10 c. water
1 T. cooking wine or sherry
2 green onions
2 slices of ginger root

3 T. soy sauce
1 1/2 t. ea: vinegar, sugar,
  hot chili paste, sesame oil
1 T. minced garlic

豬前腿肉 ⋯⋯⋯⋯⋯⋯⋯⋯12兩

水 ⋯⋯⋯⋯⋯⋯⋯⋯⋯⋯10杯
酒 ⋯⋯⋯⋯⋯⋯⋯⋯⋯⋯1大匙
蔥 ⋯⋯⋯⋯2枝，薑⋯⋯⋯⋯2片

醬油露或醬油 ⋯⋯⋯⋯⋯3大匙
糖、醋、辣椒醬、麻油 各1 $\frac{1}{2}$ 小匙
蒜末（剁細） ⋯⋯⋯⋯⋯1大匙

1 Cover pork with **1**. Bring to boil; cook for 30 minutes over medium heat. Remove pork, retain liquid. Slice pork after it cools. Pour **2** over sliced pork.

☐ Retained liquid may be used as stock. Hot chili may be purchased at most Chinese markets.

1 豬肉放入 **1** 料內（水需淹蓋肉面為宜），燒開改中火煮30分鐘，撈出待涼切薄片，淋上 **2** 料即成。

☐ 喜熱食者，食前可將肉片放入肉湯內川燙撈出，再淋上 **2** 料即成。剩下的肉湯可做其他用途。

Fig. 1

Fig. 2

Fig. 3

Crispy Fried Walnuts

糖酥核桃

½ lb (225g) shelled walnuts
  or cashews

1 c. water, 3 T. sugar
1 T. maltose or honey

oil for deep-frying

核桃（或腰果）…………6兩

水…………………………1杯
糖…………………………3大匙
麥芽糖或蜂蜜……………1大匙

「炸油」…………………適量

1. Put nuts in **1** and heat for 5 minutes over medium heat; remove and drain.

2. Heat oil. Deep-fry nuts over low heat 5 minutes. Stir continuously to prevent burning. Remove, place on paper towel. Nuts should be crispy when cool.

☐ Shell walnuts (Figs. 1 & 2). If walnuts with skin are used, they become very dark during frying. To remove the skin, blanch in boiling water then pick off with a toothpick (Fig. 3).

☐ **CRISPY FRIED CASHEWS:** follow above directions, except deep-fry cashews for 15 minutes.

1 核桃加 **1** 料以中火燒煮5分鐘撈出，瀝乾水份。

2 「炸油」燒溫熱，入核桃以小火將核桃炸酥約5分鐘（炸時需常常攪動）顏色呈淡茶色時撈出；置紙巾上便於吸油，涼後即酥脆。

☐ 買的核桃，先去外殼（圖1、圖2）如果外面有一層膜，則炸出來顏色較黑，如喜愛淡色則用開水沖泡後，用牙籤挑去膜後再使用（圖3）。

☐ **糖酥腰果：**做法與糖酥核桃相同，祇是炸的時間較長約15分鐘。

Five Spice Fish

薰魚

1 whole fish, 1 ⅓ lbs (600g)

2 green onions, cut into
  sections
2 slices of ginger root
1 T. soy sauce, ¼ t. salt
five-spice powder or pepper
  as desired

oil for deep-frying

1 red hot chili, 2 c. water
2 T. ea: sugar, soy sauce
2 T. cooking wine, 1 t. vinegar

1 T. sesame oil

魚1隻…………………1斤

醬油…………………1大匙
鹽……………………¼小匙
五香粉或胡椒………隨意
蔥（略切）…2支，薑…2片

「炸油」…………………適量

辣椒…………………1條
水……2杯，醋………1小匙
醬油、酒、糖………各2大匙

麻油…………………1大匙

1. Clean fish and pat dry. Cut into 1" (2cm) slices. Marinate with **1** 2 hours. Remove, pat dry to rid excess marinade.

2. Heat oil. Deep-fry 2 or 3 fish slices per batch 8 minutes; remove.

3. Bring **2**, fried fish, green onions and ginger (from marinade) to boil. Turn heat to medium and cook 15 minutes. Drizzle with sesame oil. Turn fish over and continue to cook until liquid completely evaporates. Let cool; serve.

☐ Carp, small yellow fish, or pomfret may be used.

1 魚拭乾水份，切2公分厚片，調 **1** 料醃2小時，炸時拭乾水份。

2 「炸油」燒熱，為防止魚片粘在一起，可分數次炸約8分鐘以上至略乾。

3 將 **2** 料、炸好的魚片及醃魚用蔥薑一同置鍋內，燒開後改中大火燒煮15分鐘至汁呈濃狀，淋上麻油，輕輕翻面再將汁烙乾，取出待冷分次食用，可做酒肴或便當菜

☐ 小黃魚、鮊魚、鯪魚、肉鯽均可做薰魚的材料。

Fig. 1

Fig. 2

Fig. 3

Beef Shanks

五香牛肉

2 lbs (900g) beef shanks, (Fig. 1)

5 c. water, ¹/₂ c. soy sauce
1 T. cooking wine
¹/₂ star anise (see Fig. 3, P. 4)

3 T. sugar
1 T. sesame oil

牛腱（圖1）⋯⋯⋯⋯⋯1斤半
水⋯⋯⋯⋯⋯⋯⋯⋯⋯5杯
醬油⋯⋯⋯⋯⋯⋯⋯⋯¹⁄₂杯
酒⋯⋯⋯⋯⋯⋯⋯⋯⋯1大匙
八角（見4頁、圖3）⋯⋯¹⁄₂朶
糖⋯⋯⋯⋯⋯⋯⋯⋯⋯3大匙
麻油⋯⋯⋯⋯⋯⋯⋯⋯1大匙

1 Cook shanks in **1**; bring to boil. Reduce heat to medium and cook 2 hours, or until tender (turn over during cooking). Use a chopstick to test for doneness. Add sugar and increase heat; turn meat until liquid thickens slightly. Add sesame oil; remove and allow to cool (Fig. 2). To serve, slice the desired portion into thin slices. Add chopped green onions, coriander, sesame oil and hot bean paste as desired. Refrigerate unused portion for later use.

1 牛腱加**1**料燒開，改中火煮約2小時（需翻面）至筷子可將肉插透，加糖以大火邊煮邊翻面煮至汁略收乾呈濃稠狀，再加麻油撈出（圖2），待冷切片，並隨意撒上蔥花、香菜、麻油及辣豆瓣醬食用；燒好之牛肉可置冰箱內，隨時取用。

Salty Chicken

白切鴨

1 chicken, 3 ¹/₃ lbs (1500g)
1 t. salt
1 T. cooking wine

1 T. soy sauce
1 T. minced garlic

鴨或鷄1隻⋯⋯⋯⋯⋯2斤半
鹽⋯⋯⋯⋯⋯⋯⋯⋯⋯1小匙
酒⋯⋯⋯⋯⋯⋯⋯⋯⋯1大匙
醬油、蒜末⋯⋯⋯⋯各1大匙

1 Put whole chicken in boiling water (water must cover chicken), bring to another boil over high heat. Remove scum. Cook 40 minutes over low heat, remove frorn pot. Spread salt and cooking wine over chicken while hot. When cooled, cut into pieces, serve with **1**.

☐ May save broth for other uses.

1 將整隻鴨放入滾水內（水需蓋過鴨身）大火煮開，去除白沫，蓋鍋改小火煮40分鐘至熟即撈出，趁熱在鴨身撒上鹽，淋上酒，待冷後切塊沾**1**料食用。

☐ 可將鴨湯留做其他用途。

Fig. 1

Fig. 2

Seaweed & Egg Flower Soup

紫菜蛋花湯

2 sheets seaweed
4 eggs

6 c. stock
1 ¹/₂ t. salt

2 T. chopped green onion

紫菜	2張
鷄蛋	4個
高湯	6杯
鹽	1 ¹/₂ 小匙
蔥花	2大匙

1 Tear seaweed into 2″ (5cm) squares. Lightly beat eggs.

2 Boil **1**. Slowly add eggs in a thin stream; stir lightly and turn off heat immediately when eggs float to the top. Add seaweed. Pepper, sesame oil and chopped green onions may be added as desired.

☐ **CANNED CHICKEN BROTH:** 1 can (2 c.) contains 1 t. salt. You may substitute for **1** by adding 4 c. water and 1/2 t. salt to 1 can of chicken broth.

1 紫菜撕成5公分四方。鷄蛋打散備用。

2 將 **1** 料燒開，徐徐淋入打散的蛋汁，使其散開立即熄火，再加紫菜即成。可隨意撒上蔥花、胡椒、麻油。

☐ **鷄湯罐頭**（1罐約2杯），鹽的含量爲1小匙；如使用鷄湯罐頭1罐可再加水4杯及鹽 ¹/₂ 小匙來取代 **1** 料。

Beef Soup

牛肉羹

¹/₂ lb (225g) ground beef

1
¹/₂ T. soy sauce
¹/₂ T. cooking wine
1 T. cornstarch

¹/₂ T. minced ginger root

2 6 c. stock or water, 1 ¹/₂ t. salt

3 4 T. cornstarch, 5 T. water

4
3 T. water
3 egg whites or 2 whole eggs

5 1 c. chopped green onions & coriander

牛絞肉	6兩
醬油、酒	各 ¹/₂ 大匙
太白粉	1大匙
薑末	¹/₂ 大匙
高湯或水	6杯
鹽	1 ¹/₂ 小匙
太白粉	4大匙，水 5大匙
水	3大匙
蛋白（或全蛋2個）	3個
蔥花、香菜（略切）	共1杯

1 Marinate meat with **1**. Adding 1 T. oil to meat before stir-frying helps to separate pieces.

2 Heat 2 T. oil, stir-fry ginger and meat slices, add **2**, bring to boil. Add mixture **3** to thicken; stir (Fig. 1). When boiling, slowly add mixture **4** in a thin stream while stirring gently (Fig. 2); add **5**. Add 1/2 t. each of pepper sesame oil.

1 牛肉調 **1** 料略醃，炒前拌油1大匙，則炒時肉易分開。

2 油2大匙燒熱炒香薑末，隨入肉炒開，再入 **2** 料燒開，以調勻的 **3** 料勾成濃汁（圖1），待滾後徐徐淋入拌勻的 **4** 料（圖2），使其散開，再加 **5** 料並撒上胡椒、麻油各 ¹/₂ 小匙即成。

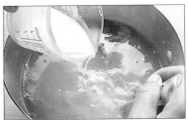
Fig. 1

Fig. 2

Casserole Soup
什錦砂鍋

6 leaves of nappa cabbage
6 bok choy
1 chicken leg

6 Chinese black mushrooms
3 dried scallops
1 ½ oz (51g) package bean
   threads

2 c. tofu, cut into pieces
10 ea: shrimp, fish balls
1 c. asparagus
1 c. mushrooms

6 c. stock, 1 ½ t. salt

1 Cut cabbage into 2″ (5cm) pieces (Fig. 1). Use only the heart and tender leaves of bok choy; trim the thick stem (Fig. 2). Cut chicken leg into pieces. Separately blanch cabbage, bok choy and chicken. Soak **1** in water to soften (Fig. 3).

2 Place cabbage in a heatproof dish; add all remaining ingredients. Stock in **2** should cover the ingredients. Bring to boil; turn heat to low and cook 20 minutes. Serve.

☐ Meat balls, abalone, squid, sea cucumber, other vegetables may be added. Fish balls may be purchased at most Chinese markets.

大白菜 ·················6片
青江菜 ·················6棵
雞腿 ···················1隻

香菇 ···················6朵
干貝 ···················3個
粉絲（小）···············1把

豆腐（切塊）·············2杯
蝦、魚丸 ···············各10個
蘆筍、毛菇 ·············各1杯

高湯 ·······6杯，鹽······1 ½ 小匙

1 大白菜切塊（圖1），青江菜取嫩莖（圖2），雞腿剁塊分別在滾水內川燙；將 **1** 料（圖3）分別泡軟。

2 砂鍋內先放入白菜，上置其他材料並倒入 **2** 料至滿過材料，燒開後改小火續煮20分鐘，用餐時可將砂鍋一齊端出。

☐ 砂鍋材料除上述外，亦可用肉丸、豬肚、鮑魚、魷魚、海參或其他蔬菜。

Crab Meat with Asparagus Soup
蟹肉蘆筍湯

total of 4 c.: crab meat, tofu
   asparagus, button
   mushrooms, (all diced)
   and peas

6 c. stock, 1 ½ t. salt

4 T. cornstarch, 5 T. water

2 T. water, 2 egg whites

1 Bring **2** to boil. Add **1** and bring to boil again. Add mixture **3** to thicken; stir. When boiling, slowly add **4** in a thin stream; stir lightly and turn off heat immediately. Pepper and sesame oil may be added as desired.

☐ Canned crab meat, canned or fresh button mushrooms and asparagus may be used. Use cooking wine and pepper to remove the seafood odor.

蟹肉、蘆筍丁、洋菇丁
   豆腐丁、青豆仁 ··········共4杯

高湯 ···················6杯
鹽 ···················1 ½ 小匙

太白粉 ·················4大匙
水 ···················5大匙

水 ···················2大匙
蛋白 ···················2個

1 將 **2** 料燒開，隨入 **1** 料再燒開，以調勻的 **3** 料勾成濃汁，待滾後徐徐淋入拌勻的 **4** 料，使其散開立即熄火，可隨意撒上胡椒、麻油即成。

☐ 蟹肉可用人造或蟹罐頭，或使用其他海鮮取代，海鮮內加少許酒及胡椒可去除腥味；毛菇、蘆筍可用罐頭或新鮮。

Fig. 1

Fig. 2

Fig. 3

Hot & Sour Soup

酸辣湯

1 Marinate meat with **1**. Beat eggs lightly.

2 Boil **2**; put in meat and stir to separate. Add tofu and bring to boil. Add mixture **3**; stir. When boiling, slowly add eggs in a thin stream; stir lightly. Add **4**; stir and serve.

☐ To enhance soup flavor, stir-fry shredded meat in 1 T. hot oil before putting in soup. Total 2 cups of shredded tofu, bamboo shoots (Fig. 1) and dried tiger lily blossoms (soaked and softened) (Fig. 2), wood ears and Chinese black mushrooms (Fig. 3), (soaked, softened and shredded) may be used in place of 2 cups of tofu.

1 肉絲調 **1** 料略醃。蛋打散備用。

2 將 **2** 料燒開，隨入肉絲攪散，續加豆腐再燒開，以調勻的 **3** 料勾成濃汁，待滾徐徐淋入打散的蛋汁，使其散開，加 **4** 料即成。

☐ 如用油1大匙燒熱，將肉絲炒至變色，再放入湯內，其湯味更香濃。湯內可加些筍絲（圖1）、木耳絲、金針菜（圖2）、香菇絲（圖3）或其他蔬菜。木耳、金針菜、香菇使用前均需泡水至軟。

2 c. shredded tofu
²/₃ c. shredded pork, beef, or chicken

1 t. cooking wine
1 t. ea: soy sauce, cornstarch

6 c. stock, 1 ¹/₄ t. salt

4 T. cornstarch, 5 T. water

2 eggs

3 T. ea: soy sauce, vinegar
total of 4 T.: chopped coriander, shredded green onion and ginger root
1 t. ea: pepper, sesame oil

豆腐（切絲）⋯⋯⋯⋯⋯⋯2杯
肉絲（豬、牛或鷄）⋯⋯⋯ ²⁄₃杯

醬油、酒⋯⋯⋯⋯⋯⋯各1小匙
太白粉⋯⋯⋯⋯⋯⋯⋯⋯1小匙
高湯⋯⋯⋯⋯⋯⋯⋯⋯⋯6杯
鹽⋯⋯⋯⋯⋯⋯⋯⋯1 ¹⁄₄小匙
太白粉⋯⋯4大匙，水⋯⋯5大匙
蛋⋯⋯⋯⋯⋯⋯⋯⋯⋯⋯2個
醬油、醋⋯⋯⋯⋯⋯⋯各3大匙
蔥、薑絲、香菜末⋯⋯⋯共4大匙
胡椒、麻油⋯⋯⋯⋯⋯各1小匙

⋯⋯⋯⋯⋯⋯

Tomato & Egg Flower Soup

番茄蛋花羹

1 Heat 1 T. oil in wok, stir-fry **1**. Add 1 T. soy sauce, stir lightly then add **2**; bring to boil. Add mixture **3** to thicken; stir. When boiling, slowly add eggs in a thin stream; stir lightly and turn off heat immediately; serve. Add dash of pepper and sesame oil as desired.

1 油1大匙燒熱，先炒 **1** 料，隨入醬油1大匙略炒，再加 **2** 料燒開，以調勻的 **3** 料勾成濃汁，待滾徐徐淋入打散的蛋汁，使其散開立即熄火，可隨意撒上胡椒、麻油即成。

1 large tomato, diced
1 T. chopped green onion

1 T. soy sauce

6 c. stock, 1 t. salt
2 c. diced tofu

4 T. cornstarch, 5 T. water

2 eggs, lightly beaten

大番茄（切丁）⋯⋯⋯⋯⋯1個
蔥花⋯⋯⋯⋯⋯⋯⋯⋯⋯1大匙
醬油⋯⋯⋯⋯⋯⋯⋯⋯⋯1大匙
高湯⋯⋯⋯⋯⋯⋯⋯⋯⋯6杯
鹽⋯⋯⋯⋯⋯⋯⋯⋯⋯⋯1小匙
豆腐（切丁）⋯⋯⋯⋯⋯⋯2杯
太白粉⋯⋯⋯⋯⋯⋯⋯⋯4大匙
水⋯⋯⋯⋯⋯⋯⋯⋯⋯⋯5大匙
蛋（打散）⋯⋯⋯⋯⋯⋯⋯2個

Fig. 1

Fig. 2

Fig. 3

Fried Chicken

炸鷄塊

1⅓ lbs (600g) chicken legs

¾ t. salt, dash of pepper
1 egg

4 T. cornstarch
oil for deep-frying

鷄腿3隻 ……………………1斤

鹽 ………………………¾小匙
胡椒 ……………………少許
蛋 ………………………1個

太白粉 …………………4大匙
「炸油」 …………………適量

1 Cut chicken legs into large pieces and marinate in **1** for at least 1 hour. Coat with cornstarch before deep-frying.

2 Heat wok then add oil. Deep-fry chicken until outside is crisp. Reduce heat to medium and continue to fry 7 minutes until done: remove and drain. If skin is not crispy, reheat oil and fry again.

☐ If chicken legs are marinated in refrigerator, increase deep-frying time to 12 minutes. Small chicken legs or chicken wings may be used to eliminate the procedure of cutting pieces.

1 鷄腿剁塊，調入 **1** 料，醃置60分鐘以上，炸前沾太白粉。

2 「炸油」燒熱，放入鷄塊炸至表面略乾，改中火再炸約7分鐘至熟撈出，若鷄皮不酥，續將油燒熱，重入鷄塊，炸至鷄皮酥脆即撈起。

☐ 醃好的鷄塊若是由冰箱取出，炸的時間約需12分鐘。利用小鷄腿或鷄翅可省去剁塊的麻煩。

Chicken Croquettes

鷄絨玫瑰

½ lb (225g) chicken breasts

½ T. ea: water, wine
¼ t. salt

4 egg whites, beaten
1 T. cornstarch
4 radishes, sliced

1 c. stock, ½ t. salt
½ T. ea: cornstarch, wine

12 molds

鷄柳或鷄胸肉 …………………6兩

水、酒 ………………各½大匙
鹽 ………………………¼小匙

蛋白（打散）………………4個
太白粉 …………………1大匙
小紅蘿蔔（切片）………………4個

高湯 ………………………1杯
鹽 ………………………½小匙
太白粉、酒 ……………各½大匙

小酒杯 …………………12個

1 Remove chicken tendons (Fig. 1). Finely chop chicken, then add **1**. Gradually pour egg whites and mix into chicken (Fig. 2). Add cornstarch and mix.

2 Oil molds then put 1 portion of chicken mixture into each mold. Arrange radish slices as shown (Fig. 3). Steam 6 minutes over low heat; remove mixture from molds. Boil **2**; stir then pour over croquettes and serve.

1 鷄柳肉去筋（圖1），剁成泥，調入 **1** 料後加蛋白，邊加邊攪拌（圖2），再加太白粉拌勻即爲「鷄絨」。

2 杯內塗油，放進鷄絨，用蘿蔔片插成花朵狀（圖3）。水燒開，用小火蒸約6分鐘即取出；將 **2** 料攪拌燒滾成薄汁淋上即成。

Fig. 1

Fig. 2

Fig. 3

Chicken Breasts With Ketchup

茄汁鷄脯

2/3 lb (300g) chicken breast

3/4 T. soy sauce
3/4 T. cooking wine
1 T. cornstarch

1 shredded onion

2 T. water, 1/2 t. cornstarch
1 1/2 T. ea: soy sauce, ketchup
1/2 T. ea: sugar, vinegar

鷄胸肉（無皮）⋯⋯⋯⋯⋯8兩

醬油、酒 ⋯⋯⋯⋯⋯各 3/4 大匙
太白粉 ⋯⋯⋯⋯⋯⋯⋯⋯1大匙

洋蔥（切絲）⋯⋯⋯⋯⋯1個

水⋯⋯⋯⋯⋯⋯⋯⋯⋯⋯2大匙
醬油、番茄醬⋯⋯⋯⋯各1 1/2 大匙
糖、醋⋯⋯⋯⋯⋯⋯⋯各 1/2 大匙
太白粉⋯⋯⋯⋯⋯⋯⋯ 1/2 小匙

1 Laterally cut chicken breasts into large pieces. Use a meat mallet to tenderize meat; add **1** and mix together.

2 Heat 2 T. oil. Briefly stir-fry onion; place on plate. Wipe wok dry. Heat 2 T. oil. Fry chicken until both sides are golden. Add **2** and stir to mix well. Remove and put on top of the onion or on the side.

☐ **TO BONE CHICKEN BREASTS:** Cut meat along outside of rib cage to the spine (Fig. 1). Spread meat away from bone (Fig. 2). Repeat for other side. Turn breast over and remove bone.

1 鷄胸肉切大片，用刀背搥鬆，調入 **1** 料拌勻。

2 油2大匙燒熱，將洋蔥略炒置盤，擦乾鍋面；另加油2大匙燒熱，將鷄片煎至兩面呈金黃色肉熟，隨入調勻的 **2** 料翻拌，盛於洋蔥上或洋蔥旁。

☐ **鷄胸去骨：**由關節處下刀切斷筋（圖1）拉開（圖2），兩邊做好一齊拉開，就可以把鷄胸骨輕易取出。

Almond Chicken

杏仁鷄片

2/3 lb (300g) chicken breast

1/2 T. cooking wine
1/2 t. ea: sugar, salt
1 egg white
2 T. cornstarch

1 1/2 c. sliced almonds or sesame seeds
oil for deep-frying

鷄胸肉（無皮）⋯⋯⋯⋯⋯8兩

酒 ⋯⋯⋯⋯⋯⋯⋯⋯⋯ 1/2 大匙
鹽、糖 ⋯⋯⋯⋯⋯⋯各 1/2 小匙
蛋白⋯⋯⋯⋯⋯⋯⋯⋯⋯1個
太白粉⋯⋯⋯⋯⋯⋯⋯⋯2大匙

杏仁片或芝麻⋯⋯⋯⋯⋯1 1/2 杯
「炸油」⋯⋯⋯⋯⋯⋯⋯適量

1 Remove skin from chicken. Cut chicken breast into 1/4″ (.5cm) slices; add **1** and mix. Coat each slice with almonds.

2 Heat oil for deep-frying; fry chicken 1 1/2 minutes until crispy. Remove and serve.

1 鷄肉切成0.5公分大薄片，與 **1** 料拌勻，兩面沾裹杏仁片。

2 「炸油」燒熱，將鷄片炸約1分半鐘至外皮酥脆，即可撈起盛盤。

Fig. 1

Fig. 2

Stir-Fried Chicken

炒鷄丁

1 Dice chicken and mix with **1**. Add 1 T. oil before stir-frying to separate meat.

2 Heat 1 T. oil. Briefly stir-fry **2** and 1 T. water; remove. Wipe wok dry. Heat 2 T. oil, stir-fry green onions and ginger root, then add chicken and fry until cooked. Add **2** and mixture **3** ; stir-fry until mixed well.

☐ **TO BONE CHICKEN LEGS:** Make vertical cut from bottom of leg to top (Fig. 1). Cut through joint. Remove meat from bone. Cut off both bones (Figs. 2 & 3).

1 鷄肉切丁，調入 **1** 料，炒前拌油1大匙，則炒時肉易分開。

2 油1大匙燒熱，將 **2** 料加水1大匙略炒撈出，擦乾鍋面；油2大匙燒熱，炒香蔥薑，隨入肉丁炒至肉變色，再加炒好的 **2** 料及調勻的 **3** 料炒拌均勻即成。

☐ **鷄腿去骨：** 在中間直劃刀（圖1）在關節處把筋切斷，把二段中間骨切除（圖2、3）。

½ lb (225g) boneless chicken legs

½ T. soy sauce
½ T. cooking wine
1 T. cornstarch

6 slices green onion
6 slices ginger root

Total of 2 c. (sliced):
mushrooms, cooked carrot, green pepper, red hot chili

3 T. water, 1 t. cornstarch
⅓ t. ea: salt, sugar
1 t. cooking wine

鷄腿肉 ·················· 6兩

醬油、酒 ·········· 各½大匙
太白粉 ·················· 1大匙

蔥、薑 ················· 各6片

洋菇、熟紅蘿蔔
　青椒、紅辣椒········ 切片共2杯

水 ··················· 3大匙
鹽、糖 ············ 各⅓小匙
酒、太白粉 ········· 各1小匙

·············

Chicken Wings

雙冬扒鷄翼

1 Cut chicken wings at joints into 3 pieces. Sprinkle on 1/2 T. of flour or cornstarch to avoid splattering during deep-frying.

2 Heat 2 T. oil, then fry chicken until both sides are golden. Put to side of wok and stir-fry **1**. Set aside.

3 Bring **2** to boil, add chicken wings and **1**, cook in high heat 15 minutes until sauce thickens. Sesame oil may be added as desired.

1 鷄翼由關節處剁開成三節；鷄翼撒½大匙的太白粉或麵粉，以免油爆。

2 油2大匙燒熱，將鷄翼煎至兩面呈金黃色，鏟於鍋邊，入 **1** 料略炒備用。

3 將 **2** 料燒開，放入煎好的鷄翼及 **1** 料，大火燒煮15分鐘至汁呈濃稠狀，可隨意加入麻油即成。

---

1 lb (450g) chicken wings

total of 2 c. (cut in pieces):
Chinese black mushrooms (softened in water), bamboo shoots, green onions

2 c. water, 4 T. soy sauce
½ T. ea: cooking wine, sugar

鷄翼 ················· 12兩

香菇（泡軟切塊）
　筍（切塊）、蔥段········ 共2杯

水 ··················· 2杯
醬油 ·················· 4大匙
酒、糖 ············ 各½大匙

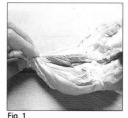

Fig. 1

Fig. 2

Fig. 3

Spicy Chicken

五味鷄

1 Mix **1** then rub on skin and in chicken cavity. Marinate 2 hours. Place chicken in pot and half cover with water. Bring to boil over high heat. Turn heat to low; cover and cook 40 minutes. Turn chicken during cooking; remove and let cool. Spread egg yolks on chicken and coat with cornstarch.

2 Heat oil. Deep-fry chicken over high heat 12 minutes, until skin is crispy; drain. Cut chicken into bite-size pieces; pour mixture **2** on chicken; serve.

☐ **TO CUT CHICKEN:** Remove wings and legs (Fig. 1). Separate breast and back (Fig. 2). Cut large pieces into bite-size pieces (Fig. 3).

1 將 **1** 料塗抹鷄身內外，醃2小時。鍋內放入鷄及水（水略蓋滿鷄身），大火燒開後，改小火煮40分鐘（中途需翻面），取出後塗抹蛋黃再沾裹太白粉。

2 「炸油」燒熱，放入鷄，大火炸約12分鐘至外皮酥脆撈起，剁塊後淋上拌好的 **2** 料即成。

☐ 剁鷄：將鷄腿、鷄翼切下（圖1），鷄胸與鷄背剖半（圖2），再切小塊即可（圖3）。如使用小鷄腿，可免剁塊。

Ingredients (Spicy Chicken)

- 2 2/3 lbs (1200g) whole chicken (or legs)
- **1** 2 t. ea: salt, cooking wine
- 2 egg yolks, 1/2 c. cornstarch
  oil for deep-frying
- **2** 3 T. soy sauce
  4 T. chopped garlic, green onions, ginger root
  1 T. ea: sugar, vinegar, water
  chopped coriander, sesame oil, ret hot chili as desired

- 鷄1隻 ························· 2斤
- **1** 鹽、酒 ····················· 各2小匙
- 蛋黃 ························· 2個
  太白粉 ························· 1/2杯
  「炸油」 ····················· 適量
- **2** 醬油 ························· 3大匙
  糖、醋、水 ················· 各1大匙
  蔥、薑、蒜末 ············· 共4大匙
  香菜、辣椒末、麻油 ······· 隨意

Kung-Pao Beef

宮保牛肉

1 Slice meat; and mix with **1**. Add 1 T. oil, mix so meat separates during frying.

2 Heat 3 T. oil. Stir-fry chili peppers until almost burnt. Add green onions and meat; stir-fry until medium rare. Add mixture **2**; stir to mix well and serve.

☐ For authenticity and to enhance the meat flavor, use sufficient oil (3 T.) to stir-fry chili peppers and green onions.

1 牛肉切片調入 **1** 料，炒前加油1大匙，則炒時肉易分開。

2 油3大匙燒熱，將乾辣椒炒至略焦狀，隨入蔥及肉片炒至六分熟，再加調勻 **2** 料炒拌均勻即成。

☐ 炒乾辣椒及蔥時油需略多（3大匙），因利用其油炒出來的肉是本菜餚之特色。

Ingredients (Kung-Pao Beef)

- 2/3 lb (300g) lean beef
- **1** 3/4 T. soy sauce
  3/4 T. cooking wine
  1 T. cornstarch
- 6 dried chili peppers
  1/2 c. green onion sections or chopped onion
- **2** 2 T. ea: soy sauce, water
  1 t. ea: vinegar, sugar
  1 t. cornstarch

- 瘦牛肉 ····················· 8兩
- **1** 醬油、酒 ················· 各3/4大匙
  太白粉 ····················· 1大匙
- 乾辣椒 ····················· 6條
  蔥粒或洋蔥丁 ············· 1/2杯
- **2** 水、醬油 ················· 各2大匙
  醋、糖、太白粉 ··········· 各1小匙

Fig. 1

Fig. 2

Fig. 3

Steamed Bacon In Soy Sauce

紅燒扣肉

1⅓ lbs (600g) fresh bacon
  slab (2″, 5cm wide)
5 T. soy sauce
oil for deep-frying

1 T. cooking wine, 2 t. sugar
2 green onions
2 slices ginger root

1 Cover bacon in 6 c. water and cook over medium heat 30 minutes. Remove; pat dry. Lightly pierce skin of bacon to prevent forming bubbles while deep-frying. Rub soy sauce on skin while hot. Pat dry before deep-frying. Retain soy sauce.

2 Heat oil. Deep-fry bacon, skin side down, over medium heat until golden (cover to avoid splashing oil). Remove; let cool. Slice (Fig. 1), then pack bacon securely, skin side down, in bowl. Add **1** and retained soy sauce (Figs. 2 & 3). Steam over high heat 1 hour. Pour out and retain liquid. Invert bowl on serving plate; remove bowl. Pour retained liquid on bacon. Serve. Can be served with rice or bread.

五花肉（約5公分寬）⋯⋯⋯1斤
醬油⋯⋯⋯⋯⋯⋯⋯⋯⋯⋯5大匙
「炸油」⋯⋯⋯⋯⋯⋯⋯⋯適量

酒⋯⋯⋯⋯⋯⋯⋯⋯⋯⋯⋯1大匙
糖⋯⋯⋯⋯⋯⋯⋯⋯⋯⋯⋯2小匙
蔥⋯⋯⋯⋯⋯⋯⋯⋯⋯⋯⋯2枝
薑⋯⋯⋯⋯⋯⋯⋯⋯⋯⋯⋯2片

1 肉加水6杯（水需淹滿肉）燒開，以中火煮約30分鐘取出拭乾，用牙籤將皮插洞以免炸時肉皮起大泡，趁熱加入醬油醃泡肉皮，炸時略拭乾。

2 「炸油」燒熱，將肉下鍋（肉皮面向鍋底蓋鍋，以免油爆），用中火炸至金黃色撈起，待涼切片（圖1），排列在碗內，加入醃肉醬油及 **1** 料（圖2、3）用大火蒸60分鐘，倒出餘汁，反扣菜盤上，再淋上餘汁，可配飯或夾入割包內食用。

Stir-Fried Beef & Green Peppers

青椒牛肉絲

½ lb (225g) beef tenderloin

½ T. soy sauce
½ T. cooking wine
1 T. cornstarch

2 c. shredded bell pepper

1 T. chopped fermented
  black beans
1½ T. chopped green onion,
  ginger root, garlic

2 T. water, 1 T. soy sauce
½ t. sugar, 1 t. cooking wine
1 t. cornstarch

1 Finely shred beef across grain and mix with **1**. Add 1 T. oil and mix so meat separates easily during frying.

2 Heat 1 T. oil. Briefly stir-fry bell pepper and 1 T. water; remove. Pat wok dry, then heat 2 T. oil. Stir-fry **2** then beef until medium rare. Add mixture **3** and bell pepper. Quickly stir over high heat; serve.

☐ Ready-made black bean garlic sauce may be used for **2**.

1 牛肉逆紋切絲，調入 **1** 料，炒前拌油1大匙，則炒時肉易分開。

2 油1大匙燒熱，將青椒加水1大匙略炒撈出，擦乾鍋面，油2大匙燒熱，炒香 **2** 料，隨入牛肉炒約六分熟，再加調勻的 **3** 料及青椒炒拌均勻即成。

☐ 市面上售有蒜蓉豆豉醬，可用來取代 **2** 料。

牛肉⋯⋯⋯⋯⋯⋯⋯⋯⋯⋯6兩

醬油、酒⋯⋯⋯⋯⋯各½大匙
太白粉⋯⋯⋯⋯⋯⋯⋯⋯1大匙

青椒（切絲）⋯⋯⋯⋯⋯⋯2杯

豆豉（切碎）⋯⋯⋯⋯⋯1大匙
蔥、薑、蒜末⋯⋯⋯共1½大匙

水⋯⋯⋯⋯⋯⋯⋯⋯⋯⋯2大匙
醬油⋯⋯⋯⋯⋯⋯⋯⋯⋯1大匙
糖⋯⋯⋯⋯⋯⋯⋯⋯⋯⋯½小匙
酒、太白粉⋯⋯⋯⋯⋯各1小匙

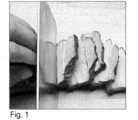
Fig. 1

Fig. 2

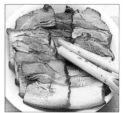
Fig. 3

Skewered Beef with Sa Tsa Chang serves 2 · 2 人份
沙茶牛肉串

2/3 lb (300g) lean beef
dash of salt, pepper

1 | **3 T. water**
6 T. (4 1/2 oz., 125g) sa tsa chang

6 skewers (8", 20cm long)

瘦牛肉 …………………… 8兩
鹽、胡椒 ………………… 適量

1 | 水 …………………………… 3大匙
沙茶醬 …………………… 6大匙

竹籤（20公分）………… 6枝

1 Cut beef in 1"x 4" (3cm x 10cm) slices. Skewer beef, sprinkle salt and pepper on both sides and place on baking pan.

2 Pre-heat oven to 450°F (235°C), bake beef 8 minutes. Remove and place on plates. Boil **1** and pour over beef; serve.

☐ Sa tsa chang may be purchased at most Chinese markets.

1 牛肉切片（3公分×10公分），用細竹籤將牛肉串起，兩面輕撒鹽、胡椒，置烤盤。

2 烤箱燒熱，以450℉烤8分鐘，即取出置盤；將 **1** 料燒開淋在烤好的牛肉串上即成。

Sweet & Sour Pork serves 2 · 2 人份
糖醋肉

1/2 lb (225g) pork

1 | **1 egg yolk, 1/2 T. soy sauce**

6 T. cornstarch
oil for deep-frying
1/2 t. chopped garlic

2 | **total of 2 c. (cut into pieces):**
onion, tomato, green pepper

3 T. ea: sugar, water, vinegar
3 | **2 T. ketchup**
1/2 t. salt, 1 1/2 t. cornstarch

瘦肉（豬、牛或雞）………… 6兩

1 | 醬油……… 1/2 大匙，蛋黃……1個

太白粉 …………………… 6大匙
「炸油」………………… 適量
蒜末 …………………… 1/2 小匙

2 | 洋蔥、青椒、番茄（切塊）共2杯

糖、醋、水 …………… 各3大匙
3 | 番茄醬 ………………… 2大匙
鹽 ……………………… 1/2 小匙
太白粉 ………………… 1 1/2 小匙

1 Cut meat into 2/3" (2cm) slices; tenderize (Fig. 1). Cut meat into bite-size pieces (Fig. 2). Mix in **1**. Dredge meat in cornstarch before deep-frying (Fig. 3).

2 Heat oil; deep-fry meat 6 minutes or until cooked and surface is crispy. Remove and drain. Remove oil from wok.

3 Heat 1 T. oil. Stir-fry garlic until fragrant. Add **2**; stir-fry briefly, add mixture **3**; stir and bring to boil. Add fried meat and toss lightly; remove and serve.

☐ Pineapple or carrot may be used for tomato in **2**.

1 肉切2公分厚片，捶鬆（圖1），切塊（圖2），調 **1** 料拌勻，炸前沾太白粉（圖3）。

2 「炸油」燒熱，入肉塊炸至表面酥脆（約6分鐘）肉熟即撈出。

3 油1大匙燒熱，炒香蒜末，入 **2** 料略炒，再加拌勻的 **3** 料燒開，放入炸過的肉塊拌炒均勻即可。

☐ 可選用鳳梨或紅蘿蔔來取代 **2** 料內之番茄。

Fig. 1

Fig. 2

Fig. 3

Beef Cooked In Soy Sauce I

紅燒牛肉㈠

2 lbs (900g) brisket of beef

1 2 C. water, 6 T. soy sauce
3 T. cooking wine
2 green onions
2 slices of ginger root

1 T. sugar
1.5 oz (51g) package bean
   threads

1 Cover beef in **1** and bring to boil . Reduce heat to low, cook 1 hour. Test tenderness with a chopstick. Add sugar; cook 10 minutes. Remove meat, let cool then slice. Retain liquid.

2 Blanch bean threads in boiling water.

3 Line medium-size heatproof bowl with sliced beef. Put bean threads and 1/2 c. retained beef stock in center of bowl (Fig. 1). Steam over high heat 20 minutes; remove. Drain liquid (Fig. 2). Invert bowl on a serving plate (Fig. 3). Remove bowl and pour retained liquid over beef; serve.

牛肋條或牛腩 ⋯⋯⋯⋯⋯⋯ 1斤半

1 水 ⋯⋯⋯⋯⋯⋯⋯⋯⋯⋯⋯⋯⋯ 2杯
醬油 ⋯⋯⋯⋯⋯⋯⋯⋯⋯⋯⋯ 6大匙
酒 ⋯⋯⋯⋯⋯⋯⋯⋯⋯⋯⋯⋯ 3大匙
蔥 ⋯⋯⋯⋯ 2枝，薑 ⋯⋯⋯⋯ 2片

糖 ⋯⋯⋯⋯⋯⋯⋯⋯⋯⋯⋯⋯ 1大匙
粉絲（小） ⋯⋯⋯⋯⋯⋯⋯⋯ 1把

1 將整塊肉放入 **1** 料內燒開，蓋鍋改小火煮60分鐘至筷子能插入肉時，再加糖續煮10分鐘撈出，稍涼後切片，湯汁留用。

2 粉絲泡軟備用。

3 將牛肉片排於碗底，上置粉絲並淋入 $\frac{1}{2}$ 杯的湯汁（圖1），蒸20分鐘；先瀝出湯汁（圖2），倒扣在盤內，再淋上湯汁即成（圖3）。

Chop Suey

炒雜碎

total of 1/2 lb (225g) shelled shrimp and lean meat

1 1/4 t. salt, 1 T. cooking wine
1 T. cornstarch

2 1 T. shredded ginger root
1 T. shredded green onion
2 black mushrooms, pre-
   softened in water, shredded

3 total of 3 c.: bean sprouts,
   shredded celery and carrots

4 3 T. water, 1 t. cooking wine
1 t. cornstarch
1/3 t. ea: salt,sugar

1 Prepare shrimp (Step 1, p.55). Shred meat; marinate with shrimp and **1** .

2 Heat 1 1/2 T. oil. Add **3** and 2 T. water; stir lightly, remove, then discard liquid. Wipe wok dry. Add 2 T. oil; stir-fry **2** until fragrant. Add shrimp and meat; stir-fry until color changes. Add **3** and **4**, stir to mix well.

☐ Deep-fried bean threads may be arranged on plate, then pour "chop suey" over them. To deep-fry bean threads, see "to deep-fry won ton skin", p.11.

蝦仁、瘦肉 ⋯⋯⋯⋯⋯⋯⋯ 共6兩

1 鹽 ⋯⋯⋯⋯⋯⋯⋯⋯⋯⋯⋯ $\frac{1}{4}$ 小匙
酒、太白粉 ⋯⋯⋯⋯⋯⋯ 各1大匙

2 蔥、薑（切絲） ⋯⋯⋯⋯ 各1大匙
香菇（泡軟、切絲） ⋯⋯⋯⋯ 2朵

3 豆芽、芹菜、紅蘿蔔絲 ⋯⋯ 共3杯

4 水 ⋯⋯⋯⋯⋯⋯⋯⋯⋯⋯⋯ 3大匙
酒、太白粉 ⋯⋯⋯⋯⋯⋯ 各1小匙
鹽、糖 ⋯⋯⋯⋯⋯⋯⋯⋯ 各 $\frac{1}{3}$ 小匙

1 蝦處理法（見55頁）；肉切絲。將蝦仁及肉絲調入 **1** 料。

2 油1 $\frac{1}{2}$ 大匙燒熱，入 **3** 料及水2大匙略炒撈出（湯汁不要），擦乾鍋面另加油2大匙燒熱，炒香 **2** 料，入蝦仁及肉炒至變色，再入炒好的 **3** 料及 **4** 料拌炒均勻即可。

☐ 可用炸粉絲墊底盛盤；炸粉絲與炸餛飩皮的做法同（見11頁）。

Fig. 1

Fig. 2

Fig. 3

Stir-Fried Beef with Onions

洋蔥牛肉

½ lb (225g) sliced beef

2 c. shredded onions

2 T. shredded ginger root
shredded red hot chili as
**   desired**

3 T. soy sauce
1 T. ea: sugar, water
1 T. cooking wine

牛肉片 ···························6兩
洋蔥（切絲） ····················2杯

薑絲 ···························2大匙
辣椒絲 ·························適量

醬油 ···························3大匙
糖、酒、水 ·················各1大匙

1 Heat 3 T. oil. Stir-fry **1** briefly. Add onion, saute. Then add **2** and beef; stir-fry until color changes. Remove and serve.

☐ Pre-cut, paper-thin slices of beef may be purchased at most Chinese or Japanese markets.

1 油3大匙燒熱，將 **1** 料略炒，隨入洋蔥炒至軟，入 **2** 料燒沸，把牛肉片拌炒至熟即成。

☐ 使用市面上切好的牛肉片較方便，如太大則略切後再使用。

Pearl Balls

糯米丸子

²/₃ lb (300g) ground pork,
**   beef or chicken**

2 T. water
1 T. cooking wine
1 T. cornstarch
½ t. salt
dash of pepper

½ c. glutinous rice

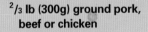

絞肉（豬、牛或雞） ···········8兩

水 ···························2大匙
酒、太白粉 ················各1大匙
鹽 ·····························½ 小匙
胡椒 ····························少許

糯米 ···························½ 杯

1 Rinse, then soak rice 1 hour; remove and drain. Stir meat and **1** until thoroughly mixed.

2 Divide and roll meat into 15 balls. Roll each ball in rice to completely coat them (Figs. 1, 2 & 3). Steam the balls in a steamer over high heat 30 minutes; remove.

☐ Chopped onions, ginger root, green onions, water chestnuts, or dried shrimp may be added to mixture. Use food coloring of preference.

1 糯米洗淨泡約1小時，瀝乾。絞肉調 **1** 料拌勻。

2 將肉餡擠成15個丸子，粘滾糯米（圖1、2、3），置於蒸盤，用大火蒸約30分鐘；如使用電鍋，則須在外鍋放1杯水。

☐ 肉餡內可加蔥、薑、洋蔥、荸薺、蝦米等。可使用食用色素將糯米丸子染成各種顏色。

Fig. 1

Fig. 2

Fig. 3

41

Beef with Broccoli In Oyster Sauce serves 2 · 2 人份

玉蘭牛肉

1 Cut meat across grain, into thin, bite-size pieces. Mix with **1**. Before frying add 1 T. oil and mix so meat separates easily during frying.

2 Separate and cut off broccoli flowerets from stem. Cook in boiling water with a dash of salt and cooking wine. Upon boiling, remove immediately and drain. Arrange flowerets around serving dish.

3 Heat 2 T. oil. Stir-fry onions, ginger root and beef until beef is cooked medium rare. Add mixture **2** ; stir to mix well and place on serving dish.

1 牛肉逆紋切薄片,調入 **1** 料,炒前拌油1大匙,則炒時肉易分開。

2 玉蘭菜分切小朵,水燒開(水需淹蓋菜,加少許鹽、油),入玉蘭菜再燒開,即撈出圍邊。

3 油2大匙燒熱,炒香蔥薑,隨入肉炒約六分熟,再加調勻的 **2** 料炒拌均勻,裝入盤內。

Ingredients (left column)

¹/₂ lb (225g) flank steak

¹/₂ T. soy sauce
¹/₂ T. cooking wine
1 T. cornstarch

²/₃ lb (300g) broccoli
6 pieces green onion,
  1" (2cm) long
6 slices ginger root

2 T. water, ³/₄ T. soy sauce
³/₄ T. oyster sauce
¹/₂ t. sugar, 1 t. cornstarch
1 t. cooking wine

瘦牛肉⋯⋯⋯⋯⋯⋯⋯⋯6兩

醬油、酒 ⋯⋯⋯⋯⋯各½大匙
太白粉⋯⋯⋯⋯⋯⋯⋯1大匙

玉蘭菜⋯⋯⋯⋯⋯⋯⋯8兩
蔥、薑⋯⋯⋯⋯⋯⋯各6片

水⋯⋯⋯⋯⋯⋯⋯⋯⋯2大匙
醬油、蠔油 ⋯⋯⋯各¾大匙
糖⋯⋯⋯⋯⋯⋯⋯⋯⋯½小匙
酒、太白粉⋯⋯⋯⋯各1小匙

⋯⋯⋯⋯⋯⋯

6 pork chops, 1 ¹/₃ lbs (600g)

1 egg
¹/₂ t. ea: salt, minced garlic
1 T. soy sauce, ¹/₂ T. sugar
dash of pepper

4 T. cornstarch

2 T. ea: soy sauce, water
1 T. ea: vinegar, sugar
Total of 2 T.: minced green
  onion, ginger root and garlic

oil for deep-frying

排骨6片 ⋯⋯⋯⋯⋯⋯⋯1斤

醬油⋯⋯⋯⋯⋯⋯⋯⋯1大匙
鹽、蒜末 ⋯⋯⋯⋯各½小匙
糖 ⋯⋯⋯⋯⋯⋯⋯⋯½大匙
胡椒或五香粉 ⋯⋯⋯⋯少許
蛋⋯⋯⋯⋯⋯⋯⋯⋯⋯1個

太白粉⋯⋯⋯⋯⋯⋯⋯4大匙

醬油、水⋯⋯⋯⋯⋯各2大匙
糖、醋⋯⋯⋯⋯⋯⋯各1大匙
蔥、薑、蒜末⋯⋯⋯共2大匙

「炸油」⋯⋯⋯⋯⋯⋯適量

Fried Pork Chops 6 pork chops · 6 人份

炸大排

1 Tenderize pork chops (Fig. 1), add **1** (Fig. 2). Marinate 1 hour. Coat with cornstarch before deep-frying (Fig. 3).

2 Heat oil. Deep-fry pork chops 4 minutes or until golden and thoroughly cooked. Remove and dip in **2**. Add chopped red chili pepper if desired.

1 排骨拍鬆,調入 **1** 料(圖1、2)醃60分鐘,炸前沾或拌入太白粉(圖3)。

2 「炸油」燒熱,將排骨炸熟至金黃色(約4分鐘),撈起置盤,食時可沾 **2** 料,辣椒末隨意。

Fig. 1

Fig. 2

Fig. 3

Chicken Legs Cooked In Soy Sauce

紅燒鷄腿

1 lb (450g) chicken legs

total of 2 c. (cut in pieces): potato, carrot & onion

2 c. water, 4 T. soy sauce
$^1/_2$ T. ea: cooking wine, sugar

1 Cut chicken into bite-size pieces. Sprinkle 1/2 T. of cornstarch or flour on chicken. Heat 2 T. oil, Fry chicken until both sides are golden, then fry **1**; set aside

2 Bring **2** to boil, add fried chicken and **1**, cook 15 minutes until sauce thickens. Add dash of sesame oil; serve.

鷄腿（切塊） ……………… 12兩
馬鈴薯、紅蘿蔔
　　洋蔥 ……………… 切塊共2杯
水 ………………………… 2杯
醬油 ……………………… 4大匙
酒、糖 ………………… 各$\frac{1}{2}$大匙

1 油2大匙燒熱，將鷄腿撒$\frac{1}{2}$大匙的太白粉或麵粉，與 **1** 料分別煎至兩面呈金黃色備用。

2 將 **2** 料燒開，放入煎好的鷄腿及 **1** 料，大火燒煮15分鐘至汁呈濃稠狀，可隨意加入麻油即成。

Stir-Fried Chicken & Vegetables

溜鷄片

$^1/_2$ lb (225g) chicken breasts

$^1/_4$ t. salt, 1 T. cornstarch
1 T. cooking wine

6 pieces green onion, 1" (2cm) long

total of 2 c.: dried wood ears, black mushrooms (both pre-softened in water), Chinese pea pods & celery

$^3/_4$ c. water, $^1/_2$ T. cornstarch
$^1/_2$ T. cooking wine
$^1/_2$ t. ea: sugar, salt

1 Slice chicken (Fig. 1); mix with **1**. Add 1 T. oil to separate meat before stir-frying. Remove string from pea pods (Fig. 2). Slice celery diagonally (Fig. 3).

2 Heat 2 T. oil. Stir-fry chicken until color changes. Remove chicken. Use remaining oil to stir-fry onions until fragrant. Add **2**; stir-fry briefly. Add mixture **3** and chicken; bring to boil. Remove and serve.

鷄胸肉 …………………… 6兩
鹽 ………………………… $\frac{1}{4}$小匙
酒、太白粉 …………… 各1大匙
蔥（切2公分長） ………… 6段
木耳或香菇（泡軟）
　　荷蘭豆、芹菜 ………… 共2杯
水 ………………………… $\frac{3}{4}$杯
酒、太白粉 …………… 各$\frac{1}{2}$大匙
鹽、糖 ………………… 各$\frac{1}{2}$小匙

1 肉切薄片（圖1），調入 **1** 料，炒前拌油1大匙，則炒時肉易分開；荷蘭豆折去硬筋（圖2），芹菜切片（圖3）。

2 油2大匙燒熱，入肉片炒至變色撈出，餘油炒香蔥段，入 **2** 料略炒，再加調勻的 **3** 料及肉片攪拌燒開即成。

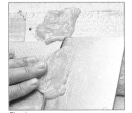

Fig. 1

Fig. 2

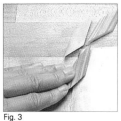

Fig. 3

Moo-Shu Pork

木須肉

1 Shred pork and mix with **1** Add 1/2 T. oil to separate meat before stir-frying.

2 Heat 1 T. oil. Stir-fry eggs until solidified; remove. Add 1 T. oil. Stir-fry spinach and bamboo shoots; add 1 T. water, stir-fry until cooked. Remove and drain.

3 Wipe wok dry. Heat 1 T. oil. Stir-fry **2** until fragrant. Add meat and stir-fry until color changes. Put in **3** and all other ingredients; toss lightly over high heat to mix; remove.

☐ Moo-shu pork may be served with rice or Moo-shu pork shells (or flour tortillas) by spreading hoisin sauce in the center (Fig. 1), topped with pork (Fig. 2), then wrapped into a roll (Fig. 3).

1 瘦肉切絲，調入 **1** 料，炒前拌油½大匙，則炒時肉易分開。

2 油1大匙燒熱，入打散的蛋液，炒至凝固鏟出；另加油1大匙，將菠菜及筍絲加水1大匙炒熟撈出，湯汁不要。

3 擦乾鍋面，加油1大匙燒熱，炒香 **2** 料，隨入肉炒至變色，再加全部材料及 **3** 料拌炒均勻即成。

☐ 可使用任何薄餅，塗抹海鮮醬，菜擺當中包捲而食（圖1、2、3），或與飯配食。

Ingredients (Moo-Shu Pork)

¹/₃ lb (150g) pork loin

1 t. soy sauce, ½ T. cornstarch
1 t. cooking wine

3 eggs, beaten
total of ²/₃ lb (300g):
    spinach (cut in 4 sections),
    shredded bamboo shoots

total of 2 T.: shredded green
    onion, ginger root
total of 1 c.: black wood ear
    & mushrooms (pre-softened
    in water & shredded)

½ T. cooking wine
1 T. soy sauce, ½ t. salt

瘦肉（豬、牛或鶏）…………4兩

醬油、酒………………各1小匙
太白粉……………………½大匙

鶏蛋…………………………3個
菠菜（切段）、筍絲……共8兩

蔥絲、薑絲……………共2大匙
香菇絲、木耳絲（泡好的）共1杯

酒……………………………½大匙
醬油………1大匙，鹽……½小匙
胡椒、麻油…………………少許

Beef Cooked In Soy Sauce II

紅燒牛肉㈡

1 Cut beef into pieces. Cook beef and **1**, turning occasionally, until all sides are seared. Add 2 c. water; bring to boil. Cover, turn heat to low and cook 50 minutes or until tender. Add **2** and cook 10 minutes, or until liquid is reduced to 2/3 cup. Add mixture **3** to thicken; stir and serve.

☐ Potatoes or carrots may be used instead of white radish.

1 牛肉切塊，盛於鍋內，加 **1** 料燒煮，燒煮時需翻動至牛肉均勻著色，再加2杯水燒開，蓋鍋改小火煮50分鐘，至牛肉熟軟，入 **2** 料續煮10分鐘至湯汁剩約⅔杯，以調勻的 **3** 料勾芡即成。

☐ 除白蘿蔔外可加馬鈴薯、紅蘿蔔。

Ingredients (Beef Cooked In Soy Sauce II)

2 lbs (900g) brisket of beef

½ c. soy sauce
2 T. cooking wine
2 green onions
2 slices ginger root
1 star anise (optional)

1 T. sugar
2 c. peeled white radish, cut
    in pieces, cooked in water

1 T. water, 2 t. cornstarch

牛腩或肋條…………………1斤半

醬油…………………………½杯
酒……………………………2大匙
蔥………2枝，薑…………2片
八角（無亦可）……………1朵

糖……………………………1大匙
白蘿蔔（切塊、煮熟）……2杯

水……………………………1大匙
太白粉………………………2小匙

Fig. 1

Fig. 2

Fig. 3

Deep-Fried Oysters

炸生蠔

2/3 lb (300g) fresh oysters

1 T. cooking wine
1/4 t. salt, 1/2 T. flour

1/2 c.flour
1 egg, beaten
1 c. bread crumbs
oil for deep-frying

1 Mix oysters with dash of salt; rinse and drain. Mix oysters with **1**.

2 Coat oysters with flour, then dip in egg. Coat oysters with bread crumbs (Figs. 1, 2 & 3).

3 Heat oil for deep-frying. Fry oysters until outside is crispy. Remove and drain. Serve with Szechuan peppercorn salt (see P. 4) or ketchup.

☐ If small oysters are used, place on skewers before coating.

1 生蠔加少許鹽，輕輕攪拌沖洗瀝乾，調入 **1** 料。

2 生蠔依序沾裹麵粉、蛋汁及麵包粉（圖1、2、3）。

3 「炸油」燒熱，放入生蠔炸至外皮酥脆撈出；沾椒鹽（見4頁）或番茄醬食用。

☐ 小的蠔可用牙籤穿串使用。

生蠔	8兩
酒	1大匙
鹽	1/4小匙
麵粉	1/2大匙
麵粉	1/2杯
蛋（打散）	1個
麵包粉	1杯
「炸油」	適量

Spicy Scallops

魚香鮮貝

1 lb (450g) fresh scallops
1 T. cooking wine, 3 T. flour

1 c. flour, 3/4 c. ice water
1/2 t. baking powder, 1 T. oil

oil for deep-frying

1 t. hot chili paste
2 T. (chopped): garlic, green onion, ginger root

6 T. water
1 1/2 t. ea: sugar, vinegar
1 1/2 t. cooking wine
1 t. ea: salt, cornstarch

1 Wash scallops and mix with cooking wine to reduce sea odor. Pat dry before frying. Mix **1**.

2 Heat oil for deep-frying. Coat scallops in flour then dip in mixture **1**. Deep-fry scallops over medium heat 3 minutes; remove.

3 Heat 2 T. oil; stir-fry **2** until fragrant. Add **3**; bring to boil then pour over scallops. Serve.

1 鮮貝洗淨調入酒，去除腥味，炸前拭乾水份。 **1** 料調成麵糊備用。

2 「炸油」燒熱，將鮮貝先沾麵粉，再沾裹麵糊炸3分鐘至外皮酥脆，撈出置盤。

3 油2大匙燒熱，炒香 **2** 料，隨入 **3** 料燒開，淋在炸好的鮮貝上即成。

新鮮干貝	12兩
酒	1大匙，麵粉 3大匙
麵粉	1杯，發粉 1/2小匙
油	1大匙，冰水 3/4杯
「炸油」	適量
蔥、薑、蒜末	共2大匙
辣椒醬	1小匙
水	6大匙
酒、糖、醋	各1 1/2小匙
鹽、太白粉	各1小匙

Fig. 1

Fig. 2

Fig. 3

Crab with Vinegar
serves 2・2 人份

燜煮蟹

3 lbs (1350g) live crab

1
- 3 T. ea: cooking wine, water
- 4 slices green onion
- 4 slices ginger root

2
- 1 T. chopped ginger root
- 3 T. vinegar, 1/8 t. salt

1 Cover and cook prepared crab and **1** over high heat until steamy. Cook 6 more minutes. Remove and serve with **2**.

☐ **TO PREPARE CRAB:** Put live crab in boiling water; cover and cook several minutes. Remove, clean and cut in pieces.

活蟹 …………………… 約2斤

1 酒、水 …………………… 各3大匙
蔥、薑 …………………… 各4片

2 醋…3大匙、薑末1大匙、鹽 1/8 小匙

1 將處理好的蟹加 **1** 料蓋鍋，大火煮至水蒸氣冒出，再煮6分鐘即撈出，沾 **2** 料食用。

☐ 活蟹處理法：可放入滾水內蓋鍋數分鐘，再拿出洗淨剁塊。

⋯⋯⋯⋯⋯⋯

---

1 whole fish, 1 2/3 lbs (750g)
3/4 t. salt

1
- 12 slices ea: pre-softened black mushrooms, green onion, lean meat, bamboo shoot

2
- 1 T. cooking wine
- 1 c. stock or water
- 1 T. sugar, 3 T. soy sauce

3
- 1/2 T. cornstarch, 1 T. water

魚1條 ………………… 1斤4兩
鹽 ………………………… 3/4 小匙

1 香菇（泡軟、切片）、蔥
瘦肉、筍 ………………… 各12片

2 醬油 …………………………… 3大匙
水……1杯，酒、糖 ……… 各1大匙

3 水……1大匙，太白粉 …… 1/2 大匙

⋯⋯⋯⋯⋯⋯

Fish Cooked In Soy Sauce
serves 2・2 人份

紅燒魚

1 Scale and clean fish; pat dry. Diagonally score both sides of fish and cut in half. Apply salt all over fish.

2 Heat 4 T. oil. Fry fish until both sides are golden; remove.

3 Stir-fry **1** with remaining oil in order listed. Return fish to wok and add **2**. Bring to boil. Reduce heat to medium; cover and cook 8 minutes, (turn over during cooking). Remove fish to platter. Add mixture **3** to remaining sauce in wok. Then pour on fish. Serve. May add sesame oil.

1 魚處理乾淨、拭乾，在二面斜劃刀，並切半比較好煎，抹上鹽備用。

2 油4大匙燒熱，將魚兩面煎黃即鏟出或鏟至鍋邊。

3 餘油把 **1** 料依序炒香後，將魚擺回鍋中加 **2** 料燒開，改中火蓋鍋煮約8分鐘（煮時需翻面），將魚鏟出置盤，餘汁以調勻的 **3** 料勾成濃汁，淋在魚上即成。麻油隨意。

2/3 lb (300g) fish meat, fillet or steak

1
- 1 T. cooking wine
- 1 T cornstarch, 1/4 t. salt

2
- 1 T. chopped fermented black beans
- 1 1/2 T. minced garlic, green onion & ginger

3 total of 1 c. (cut into pieces):
onion, green pepper

4
- 3 T. water, 1 t. cornstarch
- 1/3 t. ea: salt, sugar
- 1 t. cooking wine

魚肉 ……………………… 8兩

1 鹽 ………………………… 1/4 小匙
酒、太白粉 ……………… 各1大匙

2 豆豉（切碎）…………………… 1大匙
蔥、薑、蒜 …… 切碎共1 1/2 大匙

3 青椒、洋蔥 ………… 切塊共1杯

4 酒、太白粉 ……………… 各1小匙
水……3大匙，鹽、糖… 各1/3 小匙

Fish with Black Bean Sauce
serves 2・2 人份

豉汁魚球

1 Score fillets in crisscross fashion; cut into pieces. Mix with **1**. Add 1 T. oil to separate fish before firying.

2 Heat 3 T. oil. Stir-fry fish until color changes; remove. Use remaining oil to stir-fry **2** until fragrant. Add **3** and 1 T. water; toss lightly. Add fish and mixture **4**; stir to mix well.

1 魚肉用刀劃花紋後，切塊調入 **1** 料，炒前拌油1大匙，則炒時魚肉易分開。

2 油3大匙燒熱，放入魚塊炒至變色撈出，餘油炒香 **2** 料，隨入 **3** 料及水1大匙略炒，再加炒勻的魚塊及調勻的 **4** 料拌炒均勻即成。

Spicy Fish Fillet

瓦塊魚片

2/3 lb (300g) fish meat: fillet or steak

⃒| 1/2 T. cooking wine, 1/3 t. salt

⃒ 1 egg, 3 T. water
4 T. ea: cornstarch, flour

oil for deep-frying

⃒ 3 T. ea: chopped green onion, ginger root, garlic

⃒ 1 T. ea: cooking wine, sugar
3 T. ketchup
3/4 t. ea: hot chili paste, salt

⃒| 3/4 c. water, 1/2 T. cornstarch

1. Slice fish (Fig. 1) then marinate with **1**. Mix **2** for coating.

2. Heat oil for deep-frying. Dredge fish meat in coating (Fig. 2). Then fry until fish is thoroughly cooked and outside is crispy (Fig. 3). Remove to serving platter. Drain oil from wok.

3. Heat 2 T. oil. Stir-fry **3**, until fragrant; add **4** and stir-fry. Add mixture **5**, bring to boil then pour over fish. Serve.

1 魚肉切片（圖1）調入 **1** 料。**2** 料拌勻即為麵糊。

2 「炸油」燒熱，將魚片沾裹麵糊下鍋，炸至肉熟外皮呈金黃色（圖2、3）。

3 油2大匙燒熱，炒 **3** 料，隨入 **4** 料爆香，續入調勻的 **5** 料燒開攪拌成薄汁淋在炸好的魚片上即成。

魚肉 ················· 8兩

鹽 ········ 1/3 小匙，酒····· 1/2 大匙

太白粉、麵粉 ·············· 各4大匙
水 ··········· 3大匙，蛋········1個

「炸油」 ················· 適量

蔥、薑、蒜末 ·············· 共3大匙

番茄醬 ················· 3大匙
酒、糖 ·················· 各1大匙
鹽、辣椒醬 ·············· 各3/4 小匙

水 ····· 3/4 杯，太白粉····· 1/2 大匙

············

1 whole fish 1 lb (450g)

⃒| 1 T. cooking wine, 1 t. salt

total of 1 c.: shredded green onions, coriander
shredded baby ginger roots as desired

1/2 c. water or stock
2 T. soy sauce, 1/4 t. salt

Steamed Fish

清蒸魚

1. Clean fish then drain; apply mixture **1**. Steam fish over boiling water 10 minutes, or cook 5 to 8 minutes in microwave until done.

2. Remove fish to serving platter; discard liquid. Sprinkle **2** and drizzle 2 T. hot oil over fish. Bring **3** to boil then pour over fish. Dash of pepper as desired.

1 將魚洗淨瀝乾，拌入 **1** 料置於蒸盤內，水開用大火蒸約10分鐘，或用微波爐（視魚之大小）煮5-8分鐘至熟。

2 去魚汁，魚取出置盤，上置 **2** 料；油2大匙燒熱淋在 **2** 料上，再加燒開的 **3** 料即成。可隨意撒上胡椒。

魚1條 ···················· 12兩

酒 ······················ 1大匙
鹽 ······················ 1小匙

蔥絲、香菜
（也可加嫩薑絲）··········· 共1杯

高湯或水 ·················· 1/2 杯
醬油 ····················· 2大匙
鹽 ······················ 1/4 小匙

Fig. 1

Fig. 2

Fig. 3

Shrimp with Ketchup

乾燒蝦仁

2/3 lb (300g) shrimp, shelled

1 egg white, 1 T. cornstarch

**1/2 c. chopped onion
1/2 T. minced garlic**

**3 T. ketchup
1 T. ea: cooking wine, sugar
1 t. ea: hot chili paste, salt**

5 T. water, 1 t. cornstarch

1 **TO PREPARE SHRIMP:** Put 1 t. salt and 1 T. water on shrimp and gently mix (Fig. 1). Rinse shrimp until water is clear; drain and pat dry (Fig. 2). If large shrimp are used, cut shrimp in half. Devein shrimp (Fig. 3).

2 Mix shrimp with **1** . Add 1 T. oil to separate shrimp before stir-frying.

3 Heat 2 T. oil. Stir-fry shrimp until color changes then remove. Use remaining oil to stir-fry **2** until fragrant. Add **3** . Continue to stir-fry; add mixture **4** and shrimp. Stir-fry to mix well. Green peas may be added.

1 蝦處理法：蝦加鹽1小匙及水1大匙輕輕抓拌（圖1），漂洗數次撈出（圖2），拭乾水份，去除腸泥，大的蝦可切半使用（圖3）。

2 蝦處理後依序調入 **1** 料，炒前拌油1大匙，則炒時蝦仁易分開。

3 油2大匙燒熱，將蝦仁炒至變色撈起，餘油炒香 **2** 料，隨入 **3** 料爆香，再加調勻的 **4** 料及蝦仁拌勻，可隨意加入青豆仁略炒即成。

蝦仁	8兩
蛋白	1個
太白粉	1大匙
洋蔥（切碎）	1/2杯
蒜末	1/2大匙
番茄醬	3大匙
酒、糖	各1大匙
鹽、辣椒醬	各1小匙
水 5大匙，太白粉	1小匙

Shrimp with Vegetables

三色蝦

1/2 lb (225g) shrimp, shelled

**1/4 t. salt, 1 egg white
1 T. cooking wine
1 T. cornstarch**

**total of 2 c: green onion
pieces, tomato slices,
broccoli stem slices
(or Chinese pea pods)**

**2 T. water, 1/4 t. cornstarch
1/8 t. salt**

1 Prepare shrimp (see step 1 above). Mix shrimp with **1** . Add 1 T. oil to separate shrimp before stir-frying.

2 Heat 2 T. oil. Stir-fry shrimp until color changes then remove. Use remaining oil to stir-fry **2** and 1 T. water. Add shrimp and mixture **3** ; stir-fry to mix well.

1 蝦處理法（見上），調入 **1** 料，炒前拌油1大匙，則炒時蝦仁易分開。

2 油2大匙燒熱，入蝦仁炒至變色即撈出，餘油將 **2** 料加水1大匙略炒，隨入蝦及調勻的 **3** 料拌炒均勻即成。

蝦仁	6兩
鹽	1/4小匙
蛋白	1個
酒、太白粉	各1大匙
蔥段、番茄片	
菜心片（或豌豆莢）	共2杯
水	2大匙
鹽	1/8小匙
太白粉	1/4小匙

Fig. 1

Fig. 2

Fig. 3

Sour & Hot Shrimp

醋辣蝦

2/3 lb (300g) shrimp, shelled
1 egg white (small)
6 T. cornstarch
oil for deep-frying

1 1/2 T. ea: water, soy sauce
1 T. ea: vinegar, sugar
1 t. minced garlic
1 t. minced red hot chili

蝦仁 ································8兩
蛋白（小） ···················1個
太白粉 ···························6大匙
「炸油」 ·······················適量

水、醬油 ···············各1 $\frac{1}{2}$ 大匙
醋、糖 ·······················各1大匙
蒜、辣椒 ············切碎各1小匙

1 To prepare shrimp, see p.55. Mix with egg white, then cornstarch.

2 Heat oil for deep-frying. Fry shrimp 1 1/2 minutes until crispy, then move to side of wok. Bring **1** to boil then mix in shrimp. Remove, drain and serve.

1 蝦處理法（見55頁），加蛋白拌勻並沾裹太白粉備用。

2 「炸油」燒熱，入蝦炸約1 $\frac{1}{2}$ 分鐘至酥脆撈出。將 **1** 料燒開與炸好的蝦拌勻即成。

Shrimp Foo Yung

芙蓉蝦

1/3 lb (150g) shrimp shelled

1/8 t. salt, 1/2 egg white
1/2 T. cooking wine
1/2 T. cornstarch

total 1 c. (sliced): button
mushrooms, ham, broccoli
stem (or Chinese pea pods)

4 T. water
1/4 t. salt, 1/2 t. cornstarch
6 egg whites or 3 eggs

蝦仁 ································4兩

鹽 ································ $\frac{1}{8}$ 小匙
蛋白 ······························ $\frac{1}{2}$ 個
酒、太白粉 ··········各 $\frac{1}{2}$ 大匙

洋菇、火腿
　菜心（或豌豆莢）···切片共1杯

水 ································4大匙
鹽 ································ $\frac{1}{4}$ 小匙
太白粉 ···························· $\frac{1}{2}$ 小匙
蛋白 ································6個

1 To prepare shrimp, see p.55. Mix shrimp with **1** (Figs. 1 & 2). To help separate shrimp, add 1/2 T. oil before stir-frying (Fig. 3).

2 Heat 1 T. oil. Stir-fry shrimp until color changes; remove and set aside. Heat 1 T. oil. Stir-fry mixture **2** and 1/2 T. water. Add shrimp and mixture **3** and stir-fry. If shrimp sticks to wok, add a little more oil. Stir-fry until liquid thickens; serve.

1 蝦處理法（見55頁）；將蝦仁依序調入 **1** 料（圖1、2），炒前拌油 $\frac{1}{2}$ 大匙，則炒時蝦仁易分開（圖3）。

2 油1大匙燒熱，將蝦仁炒至變色即鏟出；油1大匙燒熱，隨入 **2** 料及水 $\frac{1}{2}$ 大匙略炒，再加炒好的蝦仁及調勻的 **3** 料（如太乾，鍋邊加少許油）拌炒至略凝固即成。

Fig. 1

Fig. 2

Fig. 3

Jumbo Shrimp with Ketchup

serves 2 · 2 人份

軟酥明蝦

6 jumbo shrimp, $^2/_3$ lb (300g)

1 T. cooking wine,
1 T. cornstarch, $^1/_8$ t. salt

$^2/_3$ c. powdered glutinous rice
7 T. water
$^1/_2$ t. baking powder

oil for deep-frying

1 $^1/_2$ T. sugar, $^1/_2$ t. salt
1 T. cooking wine
3 T. ea: ketchup, water
1 t. cornstarch, 1 T. vinegar

1 Shell shrimp, leave tail intact (Fig. 1). Wash shrimp in salt water and rinse in clear water; drain and pat dry. Cut back of shrimp in half lengthwise (Fig. 2) but do not break apart. Remove dark vein. Open shrimp, then prick inside several times (Fig. 3) so it will not curl while frying. Mix shrimp with **1**. Mix **2** to form a paste.

2 Heat oil for deep-frying. Hold each shrimp by the tail and dip in **2** then put in wok. Deep-fry until shrimp is slightly dry and crispy on the outside. Turn heat to medium. Deep-fry 5 minutes or until shrimp is crispy. Remove and drain. Remove all but 1 T. oil from wok. Add mixture **3**; bring to boil and add shrimp; stir-fry until ingredients are completely mixed. Serve.

大明蝦6隻 ⋯⋯⋯⋯⋯⋯ 8兩

鹽 ⋯⋯⋯⋯⋯⋯⋯⋯⋯ $\frac{1}{8}$小匙
太白粉、酒 ⋯⋯⋯⋯⋯ 各1大匙

糯米粉 ⋯⋯⋯⋯⋯⋯⋯⋯ $\frac{2}{3}$杯
發泡粉 ⋯⋯ $\frac{1}{2}$小匙，水 ⋯⋯7大匙

「炸油」 ⋯⋯⋯⋯⋯⋯ 適量

番茄醬、水 ⋯⋯⋯⋯⋯ 各3大匙
糖 ⋯⋯⋯ 1 $\frac{1}{2}$大匙，鹽 ⋯⋯ $\frac{1}{2}$小匙
太白粉 ⋯⋯⋯⋯⋯⋯⋯⋯ 1小匙
酒、醋 ⋯⋯⋯⋯⋯⋯⋯ 各1大匙

1 蝦去殼留尾（圖1）洗淨拭乾，由背部剖開（圖2）打開成一大片，除腸泥，在內面劃數刀（圖3，則炸時不易捲縮）。蝦調入 **1** 料，**2** 料拌勻成麵糊。

2 「炸油」燒熱，提蝦尾部沾裏麵糊，炸約5分鐘至表面酥脆即撈出。留油1大匙，入調勻的 **3** 料燒開後，再加炸蝦拌勻即成。

Stir-Fried Shrimp

serves 2 · 2 人份

清炒蝦仁

$^2/_3$ lb (300g) shrimp, shelled

$^1/_4$ t. salt, 1 T. cooking wine
1 egg white, 1 T. cornstarch

2 T. water, $^1/_4$ t. cornstarch

8 flowerets of broccoli

1 To prepare shrimp, see p.55. Devein shrimp then mix with **1**. To help separate shrimp, add 1 T. oil before stir-frying.

2 Blanch broccoli in boiling water; remove and arrange around a platter.

3 Heat 2 T. oil. Stir-fry shrimp until color changes. Add mixture **2**; stir to mix well. Remove to platter.

蝦仁 ⋯⋯⋯⋯⋯⋯⋯⋯⋯ 8兩

鹽 ⋯⋯⋯⋯⋯⋯⋯⋯⋯ $\frac{1}{4}$小匙
蛋白 ⋯⋯⋯⋯⋯⋯⋯⋯⋯ 1個
酒、太白粉 ⋯⋯⋯⋯⋯ 各1大匙

水 ⋯⋯⋯⋯⋯⋯⋯⋯⋯⋯ 2大匙
太白粉 ⋯⋯⋯⋯⋯⋯⋯⋯ $\frac{1}{4}$小匙

玉蘭菜（取花部） ⋯⋯⋯⋯ 8朵

1 蝦處理法（見55頁），依序調入 **1** 料，炒前拌油1大匙，則炒時蝦仁易分開。

2 將玉蘭菜在開水內川燙後，撈出圍邊。

3 油2大匙燒熱，將蝦仁炒至變色，隨入調勻的 **2** 料拌勻，盛入盤中即成。

Fig. 1

Fig. 2

Fig. 3

Vegetable Rolls

素菜捲

3 cabbage leaves
1/2 lb (225g) shredded white
   radish
3 oz (75g) shredded carrot

1 T. ea: sugar, vinegar
1 t. sesame oil
dash of pepper
1 T. shredded baby ginger
   root

24 shreds of red hot chili

包心菜	3片
白蘿蔔絲	6兩
紅蘿蔔絲	2兩
糖、醋	各1大匙
麻油	1小匙
胡椒	少許
嫩薑絲	1大匙
辣椒絲	適量

1 Soften radish and carrot with 1 t. salt; marinate 20 minutes. Drain and lightly squeeze out water. Mix with **1** and set aside.

2 Parboil cabbage until soft, remove and drain. Cut off stems from leaves (Fig. 1).

3 Place 2 shreds of chili, a portion of radish and carrot in each cabbage leaf, fold each end over, then roll like an egg roll. Cut each roll in half. Chopped wood ear may be sprinkled on the open ends as desired.

☐ For large quantities: Rinse cabbage. Use sharp knife to cut into and around cabbage core (Fig. 2). Place whole cabbage in boiling water. Separate leaves from core (Fig. 3).

1 紅、白蘿蔔以鹽1小匙醃20分鐘，略握乾水份，拌入 **1** 料備用。

2 包心菜放入滾水內燙軟，撈出泡冷水待涼，切除中間硬梗（圖1）。

3 每片包心菜底擺辣椒，再放入紅、白蘿蔔，將兩邊包心菜往裡折疊，再由另一邊捲成筒狀，由中間斜切成兩段，切口朝上；可隨意撒上木耳絲。

☐ 做多量時包心菜在底部劃一圈，放入滾水內再一片片撥開（圖2,3）。

Shrimp with Soy Sauce

油泡蝦

2/3 lb (300g) medium shrimp,
   with shell
1/2 T. cornstarch or flour

2 T. soy sauce
1 1/2 T. sugar
1 t. cooking wine
1 t. minced garlic

中蝦	8兩
太白粉或麵粉	$\frac{1}{2}$ 大匙
醬油	2大匙
糖	1 $\frac{1}{2}$ 大匙
酒、蒜末	各1小匙

1 Rinse shrimp then pat dry. Use scissors to cut the back of the shrimp lengthwise; do not cut through. Devein the shrimp. Sprinkle on cornstarch to eliminate excess water.

2 Heat 2 T. oil. Fry both sides of shrimp until color changes. Add **1** . Quickly stir-fry until ingredients are thoroughly mixed. Remove and serve.

1 蝦洗淨拭乾，由背部用剪刀剪開，挑出腸泥，撒上太白粉可除去多餘水份。

2 油2大匙燒熱，將蝦擺平放入鍋內兩面煎至變色，隨入 **1** 料拌勻即成。

Fig. 1

Fig. 2

Fig. 3

Stir-Fried Spinach

炒菠菜

1 Wash spinach and cut into 4 sections.

2 Heat 1 1/2 T. oil. Add spinach and **1**. Cover and cook until steamy. Stir briefly then remove.

1 菠菜洗淨，切段。

2 油1½大匙燒熱，隨入菠菜及 **1** 料蓋鍋至水蒸氣冒出略拌即成。

---

²/₃ lb (300g) spinach

¹/₃ c. water, ¹/₄ t. salt
¹/₂ T. minced garlic

菠菜 ·························· 8兩
水 ······························ ⅓杯
鹽 ······························ ¼小匙
蒜末 ···························· ½大匙

Stir-Fried Cabbage

炒高麗菜

1 Cut cabbage and tomato into bite-size pieces.

2 Heat 1 1/2 T. oil. Add **1**; stir briefly. Add **2**; cover and cook until steamy. Serve.

1 高麗菜、番茄均切塊。

2 油1½大匙燒熱，隨入 **1** 料略炒，再加 **2** 料蓋鍋至水蒸氣冒出略拌即成。

---

¹/₂ medium-size tomato
1 T. chopped green onion

²/₃ lb (300g) cabbage
3 T. water
¹/₃ t. ea: salt, sugar

中番茄 ························ ½個
蔥花 ··························· 1大匙

高麗菜 ························· 8兩
水 ···························· 3大匙
鹽、糖 ···················· 各⅓小匙

Stir-Fried Bean Sprouts

炒豆芽菜

1 Wash bean sprouts.

2 Heat 1 1/2 T. oil. Add **1** and **2**. Cover and cook until steamy. Stir-fry briefly then remove.

1 豆芽洗淨。

2 油1½大匙燒熱，隨入 **1** 料及 **2** 料蓋鍋至水蒸氣冒出略拌即成。

2/3 lb (300g) bean sprouts
1 T. chopped green onion

3 T. water
1/4 t. salt

豆芽 ··························· 8兩
蔥花 ··························· 1大匙

水 ···························· 3大匙
鹽 ···························· ¼小匙

Stuffed Tofu

箱子豆腐

1 Add **1** to meat and mix thoroughly (filling). Pat tofu dry.

2 Heat oil. Deep-fry tofu until golden; remove. Let cool. (Ready-made fried tofu may be purchased at Chinese markets). Laterally cut tofu to 1/4 thickness; do not cut through (Fig. 1). Scoop out tofu to form pocket (Fig. 2) and stuff with meat filling (Fig. 3).

3 Heat 1 T. oil. Stir-fry onions until fragrant. Add mixture **2** and tofu; cover. Cook over medium high heat 10 minutes until liquid thickens. (Turn tofu over during cooking to avoid sticking to pot). Serve.

1 絞肉調 **1** 料拌勻成餡；豆腐拭乾水份備炸。

2 「炸油」燒熱，入豆腐炸至表面呈金黃色撈起，可買現成油炸豆腐，在厚度¼處片開（圖1），但不切斷，在內面挖成凹狀（圖2），鑲入肉餡（圖3）。

3 油1大匙燒熱，炒香蔥段，隨入調勻的 **2** 料及平擺入鑲好的豆腐燒開，改中大火煮10分鐘成濃稠狀（中途需翻面，留意避免黏鍋）。

Ingredients (left column)

2 boxes tofu (8 pieces), 32 oz (900g)
oil for deep-frying
$\frac{1}{2}$ lb (225g) ground pork or beef

3 T. water
1 T. ea: cooking wine, soy sauce, cornstarch
dash of pepper

$\frac{1}{4}$ c. green onions (white part)

1 $\frac{1}{2}$ c. water, 4 T. soy sauce
1 T. sugar, $\frac{1}{2}$ T. cornstarch

豆腐2盒（8塊） ············1斤半
「炸油」 ·····················適量
豬或牛絞肉 ·····················6兩

水 ·····························3大匙
酒、醬油、太白粉 ········各1大匙
胡椒 ·····························少許

蔥白 ·····························¼杯

水 ··························1½杯
醬油 ·····························4大匙
糖······1大匙，太白粉······½大匙

············

Egg Foo Yung

芙蓉炒蛋

1 Lightly beat eggs with **1** . Devein and wash shrimp; drain.

2 Heat 2 T. oil. Stir-fry shrimp until color changes. Add onion, stir lightly; remove. Combine eggs, shrimp, onions and ham in large bowl.

3 Heat 2 T. oil. Swirl to spread oil over wok. Pour egg combination into wok and quickly stir until mixture slightly solidifies. Lightly flatten to form big pancake. If necessary, add a little more oil to prevent burning. Hold wok and move in a circular motion; cook until both sides are golden brown. Add **2** ; bring to boil. Remove and serve.

1 雞蛋加 **1** 料打勻。蝦仁去腸泥，洗淨拭乾水份。

2 油2大匙燒熱，將蝦仁炒至變色、洋蔥略炒撈出，連同火腿加入拌勻的蛋內。

3 油2大匙燒熱，輕搖使油均勻遍佈鍋面，用大火將拌好的材料拌炒稍凝固時，按扁成圓餅狀，如黏鍋由鍋邊加少許油，搖動鍋子煎至兩面呈金黃色，再加調勻的 **2** 料燒開即成。

Ingredients (Egg Foo Yung)

5 eggs

$\frac{1}{2}$ t. sugar, 1 t. salt

$\frac{1}{2}$ c. shelled shrimp
1 slice shredded ham
1 c. shredded brown onion

$\frac{2}{3}$ c. water
1 t. cornstarch

蛋 ·····························5個

糖 ·····························½小匙
鹽 ·····························1小匙

蝦仁 ·····························½杯
洋蔥（切絲）·····················1杯
火腿（切絲）·····················1片

水 ·····························⅔杯
太白粉·····························1小匙

Fig. 1

Fig. 2

Fig. 3

Tofu with Black Bean Sauce

豉汁豆腐

1 box tofu, 16 oz (450g)

2 T. chopped green onion,
  ginger root, garlic

1/4 c. any ground meat
1 1/2 T. fermented black beans

1 c. water, 3 T. soy sauce
1 T. cooking wine, 1/2 t. salt

1 T. ea: cornstarch, water

1 Cut tofu into pieces.

2 Heat 2 T. oil. Stir-fry **1** until fragrant. Add **2**, stir-fry lightly; add **3** and tofu. Bring to boil; reduce heat to medium. Cook 3 minutes. Add Chinese pea pods if desired. Add mixture **4** to thicken. Pepper and sesame oil may be added as desired.

1 豆腐切塊

2 油2大匙燒熱，炒香 **1** 料，隨入 **2** 料略炒，再加 **3** 料，及豆腐燒滾後，改中火燜煮約3分鐘（可加脆豆莢），以 **4** 料勾成薄汁即成。胡椒、麻油隨意。

豆腐1盒 ……………………12兩

蔥、薑、蒜末 ……………共2大匙

絞肉（豬、牛或雞）………1/4杯
豆豉 …………………………1 1/2大匙

水 ……………………………1杯
醬油 …………………………3大匙
鹽 ……………………………1/2小匙
酒 ……………………………1大匙

太白粉、水 ………………各1大匙

Family-Style Tofu

家常豆腐

2 pieces tofu, 8 oz (225g)
oil for deep-frying
1/3 c. any sliced meat

1/2 T. soy sauce, 1 t. cornstarch

3 pre-softened mushrooms,
  sliced
3/4 c. sliced bamboo shoot
8 slices ea: green onion,
  ginger root

1 c. water, 2 T. soy sauce
2 T. oyster sauce
1/2 T. cornstarch, 1/2 T. sugar

1 Cut tofu into 24 triangles. Pat slices dry (Figs. 1 & 2). Mix **1** with meat.

2 Heat oil for deep-frying. Deep-fry tofu pieces 2-3 minutes until golden. Remove and drain (Fig. 3). Remove oil from wok. Ready-made deep-fried tofu may be used.

3 Heat 2 T. oil and briefly stir-fry meat slices; move to side of wok. Add **2**; stir slightly. Add **3**, meat and tofu; stir 2 minutes. Pepper, sesame oil and chili pepper may be added as desired.

1 豆腐共切24片，拭乾水份（圖1、2）。肉片調 **1** 料。

2 「炸油」燒熱，將豆腐炸約2-3分鐘呈金黃色（圖3）撈起。可買現成炸豆腐取代。

3 油2大匙燒熱，放入肉片略炒鏟於鍋邊，續入 **2** 料略炒，再加 **3** 料及豆腐略翻炒煮約2分鐘，隨意加胡椒、麻油、辣椒等。

豆腐2塊 ……………………6兩
「炸油」 ……………………適量
肉片（豬、牛或雞）………1/3杯

太白粉……1小匙，醬油… 1/2大匙

蔥、薑片 ……………………各8片
香菇（泡軟切片）……………3朵
筍（切片）…………………3/4杯

水 ……………………………1杯
醬油、蠔油 …………………各2大匙
糖、太白粉 …………………各1/2大匙

Fig. 1

Fig. 2

Fig. 3

67

Steamed Egg Pudding

蒸蛋

3 eggs

2 c. water, 1 T. soy sauce
$^1/_2$ t. sesame oil or shortening
$^3/_4$ t. ea: salt, cooking wine

蛋 ································· 3個

水 ································· 2杯
醬油 ······························ 1大匙
豬油或麻油 ·················· $\frac{1}{2}$小匙
鹽、酒 ······················ 各$\frac{3}{4}$小匙

1 Beat eggs and mix with **1**. Boil water and steam egg mixture 2 minutes over high heat. Lower heat and steam 15 more minutes. If microwave is used, cook at high for 7 minutes.

☐ Test for doneness by inserting fork in center of pudding. If clean when removed, pudding is cooked. Maintain low heat and do not cover completely during steaming to prevent overcooking. Steaming and baking time may vary due to size of steaming dish. Check for doneness continually.

☐ Shrimp, clams, celery, Chinese black mushrooms, chopped green onion or garlic may be added as desired. 2 c. (1 can) chicken broth may be used for **1**.

1 蛋打散，調入 **1** 料或鷄湯一罐，水燒開蒸2分鐘，改小火續蒸15分鐘。如用微波爐需約7分鐘。

☐ 蒸蛋時可打開來看，筷子插入如無蛋液流出即可；蒸蛋容器深淺不同，花費時間不定，如蒸過久不好吃，宜用小火蒸。

☐ 材料內可酌加蝦仁、蛤蜊、芹菜、蔥末、蒜末或香菇等。

Nappa Cabbage with Tofu

白菜豆腐

$^2/_3$ lb (300g) nappa cabbage,
cut into pieces
1 c. tofu, cut into pieces

total of $^1/_2$ c.: ham (sliced),
dried shrimp (soaked and
softened), green onion
pieces

$^1/_2$ c. stock or water
$^1/_2$ t. salt, $^3/_4$ T. cornstarch

大白菜（切塊）·············· 8兩
豆腐（切塊）··················· 1杯

洋火腿（切片）
　蝦米（泡軟）、蔥段 ···共$\frac{1}{2}$杯

高湯或水 ······················ $\frac{1}{2}$杯
鹽 ································· $\frac{1}{2}$小匙
太白粉 ·························· $\frac{3}{4}$大匙

1 Heat 2 T. oil. Stir-fry **1** until fragrant. Add cabbage (Fig. 1), tofu and mixture **2** (Fig. 2). Bring to boil, stir, cover and cook over medium heat 5 minutes (Fig. 3). Remove and serve.

☐ Scallops may be substituted for dried shrimp. Clean then soak scallops in hot water for at least 1 hr. Shred scallops by hand. Retain liquid to substitute water in **2** if desired.

1 油2大匙燒熱，炒香 **1** 料，隨入大白菜（圖1）、豆腐及拌勻的 **2** 料燒開（圖2），略拌改中火蓋鍋燒煮5分鐘即成（圖3）。

☐ 亦可用干貝取代蝦米；泡干貝的水，可加入白菜內燒煮。

Fig. 1

Fig. 2

Fig. 3

Chicken, Shrimp & Vegetable Dish serves 2 · 2 人份
八寶菜

1 To prepare shrimp, see p.55. Mix shrimp and chicken breast with **1**.

2 Heat 3 T. oil. Stir-fry shrimp and chicken; remove. Stir-fry **2** & **3** with remaining oil. Cover and cook 3 minutes. Stir occasionally. Add shrimp and chicken; stir to mix well.

☐ Any kind of vegetables may be used as desired.

1 肉片與蝦仁調入 **1** 料（蝦處理法見55頁）。

2 油3大匙燒熱，放入肉片及蝦仁炒熟撈出，餘油將 **2** 、 **3** 料翻炒，蓋鍋煮約3分鐘（中途需翻拌），再加炒好的肉片及蝦仁拌勻即成。

☐ 可隨喜好選擇各種不同種類的蔬菜來烹調此菜餚。

---

²/₃ c. shelled shrimp & chicken breast slices

1 ¼ t. salt, 1 t. cornstarch

2 total of 4 c. or 1 lb (450g) (all cut in pieces): pre-softened chinese black mushrooms, carrots, nappa cabbage, broccoli, cauliflower

3 1 c. stock or water
1 T. cooking wine
1 t. ea: sugar, salt
pepper, sesame oil as desired
1 T. cornstarch

鷄胸肉（切片）、蝦仁 …共²/₃杯

1 鹽 ……………………¼小匙
太白粉 …………………1小匙

2 香菇（泡軟），大白菜、青、白花菜、紅蘿蔔…切塊共4杯（12兩）

3 水 ……………………1杯
酒、太白粉 ……………各1大匙
糖、鹽 …………………各1小匙
胡椒、麻油 ……………少許

············

**12 leaves of nappa cabbage
²/₃ lb (300g) ground meat**

1 3 T. water, 1 T. cooking wine
1 T. cornstarch, ½ t. salt

2 1 c. stock
1 ½ T. softened dry shrimps
½ T. soy sauce
½ T. cornstarch, ½ t. salt

大白菜 …………………12片
絞肉（半肥瘦肉）…………8兩

1 水 ……………………3大匙
酒、太白粉 ……………各1大匙
鹽 ……………………½小匙

2 高湯（連白菜蒸汁）………1杯
蝦米（泡軟）…………1½大匙
醬油、太白粉 ………各½大匙
鹽 ……………………½小匙

Cabbage Rolls makes 12 · 12 捲
佛手白菜

1 Parboil cabbage until soft; remove and drain. If stem is thick, cut lengthwise to make it pliable to roll (Fig. 1). Make lengthwise cuts every 1/2″ (1cm) (Figs. 2 & 3).

2 Add **1** to meat and mix thoroughly (filling). Divide into 12 portions.

3 Sprinkle cornstarch on cabbage leaf; crosswise place 1 portion of filling at one end. Roll up leaf to enclose filling. Follow same procedure for all leaves. Place the rolls on heatproof dish and steam over medium heat 12 minutes; remove. Stir and boil **2** (pepper and sesame oil may be added); pour over cabbage rolls; serve.

1 大白菜燙軟撈出瀝乾，如莖部太厚，片薄（圖1），每隔1公分直切刀痕備用(圖2、3)。

2 絞肉調入 **1** 料拌勻成餡，分成12份。

3 大白菜上撒太白粉，放入1份餡捲成佛手狀，水開後改中火蒸12分鐘取出。將調勻的 **2** 料燒開，可隨意加入胡椒、麻油，淋於白菜上即成。

Fig. 1

Fig. 2

Fig. 3

Fried Rice with Ground Beef

serves 2 • 2 人份

番茄炒飯

1 Heat 2 T. oil. Saute onions until fragrant (may add chopped garlic and chili). Add ground beef and stir until cooked. Add **1**; mix well. May add black pepper.

1 油2大匙燒熱，將洋蔥炒軟（可多加蒜及辣椒），隨入絞肉炒熟，再加 **1** 料拌炒均勻，隨意撒上胡椒即成。

Curried Fried Rice

serves 2 • 2 人份

咖哩炒飯

1 Heat 1 T. oil. Stir-fry **2** and 1 T. water, stir lightly and remove. Dry wok, add 2T. oil. When oil is hot, stir-fry meat then put on side of wok. Stir-fry onion and **1** until fragrant. Add **2**, rice and meat. Mix well; serve.

1 油1大匙燒熱，將 **2** 料加水1大匙略炒鏟出，擦乾鍋面；另加油2大匙燒熱，將肉略炒，鏟於鍋邊，依序入洋蔥及 **1** 料炒香，再加炒好的 **2** 料、飯及肉拌炒均勻即成。

Fried Rice with Eggs

serves 2 • 2 人份

蛋炒飯

1 Heat 2 T. oil. Stir-fry shrimp, when cooked add eggs and stir-fry until solidified; remove. Add 1 T. oil, stir-fry **1**, then add shrimp, eggs and **2**; mix well.

☐ **TO COOK STEAMED RICE:** If rice cooker is unavailable, rinse 1 1/4 c. rice; drain. Soak rice in 1 1/4 c. water 30 minutes. Bring to boil over high heat. Boil 1 minute. Stir, then cover; lower heat and cook 20 minutes. Turn off heat; let stand 10 minutes.

1 油2大匙燒熱，先將蝦仁炒熟，再入打勻的蛋炒至凝固鏟出；另加油1大匙，入 **1** 料略炒，隨入蝦仁、蛋及 **2** 料拌炒均勻即成。

☐ 煮飯法：1¼杯米洗淨瀝乾水，再加水1¼杯浸泡30分鐘（如煮出飯欲較乾可少加水），用大火開煮1分鐘略攪，蓋鍋蓋改小火續煮20分鐘，即熄火再燜10分鐘便可。或用電鍋煮成飯亦可。

---

¹/₃ lb (150g) ground beef, chicken or pork

1 c. chopped brown onion

2 ¹/₂ c. steamed rice, ¹/₂ t. salt
3 T. ketchup, 1 t. sugar

絞肉（豬、牛或雞）············4兩
洋蔥（切碎）·····················1杯

飯 ···································2½杯
番茄醬······························3大匙
糖 ···································1小匙
鹽 ···································½小匙

············

¹/₃ lb (150g) shredded ham or ground meat
¹/₂ c. shredded brown onion

¹/₂ T. curry powder, ¹/₂ t. salt

total of 1 c.: shredded green pepper & carrot

2 ¹/₂ c. steamed rice

火腿或絞肉····················4兩
洋蔥絲····························½杯

咖哩粉····························½大匙
鹽 ···································½小匙

青椒絲、紅蘿蔔絲··········共1杯
飯 ···································2½杯

············

2 eggs, beaten
1/3 lb (150g) shelled shrimp

total of 1 c.: peas, diced button mushrooms
2 T. chopped green onion

¹/₂ t. salt
dash of pepper
2 ¹/₂ c. steamed rice

蛋 ···································2個
蝦仁································4兩

洋菇丁、青豆仁··············共1杯
蔥花································2大匙

鹽 ···································½小匙
胡椒································少許
飯 ···································2½杯

1 $^1/_3$ lb (150g) dried noodles

1 total of $^2/_3$ c.: shelled shrimp, sliced lean pork, beef, or chicken

2 1 t. ea: soy sauce, wine
$^1/_2$ T. cornstarch

3 2 black mushrooms, sliced, pre-softened in water
6 green onion sections, 1" (2cm) long
6 slices ginger root

$^1/_2$ lb (225g) sliced nappa cabbage

4 1 $^1/_2$ c. water
1 T. ea: soy sauce, cornstarch
1 t. sugar, $^1/_2$ t. salt

1 乾麵條 ·························· 4兩

1 蝦仁、豬、牛或雞肉片 ···共$^2/_3$杯

2 醬油、酒 ···················· 各1小匙
太白粉 ·························· $^1/_2$大匙

3 香菇（泡軟、切片）·········· 2朵
蔥 ··········· 6段，薑··········· 6片

大白菜（切條）·············· 6兩

4 水 ·························· 1$^1/_2$杯
醬油、太白粉 ·············· 各1大匙
糖 ········· 1小匙，鹽········· $^1/_2$小匙

·············

$^1/_3$ lb (150g) dried noodles

1 $^1/_2$ c.: shredded or ground lean pork, beef, or chicken
total of $^1/_3$ c.: green onions $^1/_2$" (1cm) long, black mushrooms (pre-softened & shredded)

2 1 c. shredded bamboo shoot and carrot
$^1/_3$ lb (150g) spinach

3 $^1/_2$ c. water, 1 T. soy sauce
$^1/_2$ t. salt

乾麵條 ·························· 4兩

1 豬、牛或雞絲（或絞肉）···$^1/_2$杯
蔥段、香菇（泡軟、切絲）共$^1/_3$杯

2 筍絲、紅蘿蔔絲 ·············· 共1杯
菠菜 ·························· 4兩

3 水 ·························· $^1/_2$杯
醬油 ·························· 1大匙
鹽 ·························· $^1/_2$小匙

Meat, Shrimp & Noodle Platter

燴麵

1 Marinate **1** with **2**. Add 1 T. oil to help separate meat during stir-frying.

2 Heat 3 T. oil. Stir-fry **1** until color changes; remove. With remaining oil, stir-fry **3** then cabbage; add mixture **4**; stir and bring to boil. Add meat and shrimp; bring to boil again. Turn off heat. Add pepper and sesame oil as desired.

3 Cook noodles then place on plate. Pour meat mixture over noodles.

☐ **TO COOK NOODLES:** Boil a half pot of water. Put in noodles; bring to boil again, stirring gently. Depending on the type of noodles, cook in medium heat 3 to 6 minutes. 1/3 lb dried noodles equal 1 lb cooked noodles.

1 將 **1** 料與 **2** 料拌勻，炒前拌油1大匙則炒時肉易分開

2 油3大匙燒熱，將醃好的 **1** 料炒至變色鏟出，餘油將 **3** 料炒香，隨入大白菜略炒，再加 **4** 料攪拌燒開，續入炒好的 **1** 料再燒開，可隨意撒上胡椒、麻油。

3 麵煮熟盛盤，澆上煮好的湯料即可。

☐ **煮麵法：** 半鍋水燒熱，放入麵條輕攪拌，大火燒開。視麵的種類，改中火煮3-6分鐘至熟，乾麵條4兩，煮熟後增爲12兩。

Stir-Fried Noodles

炒麵

1 Cook noodles (see above recipe).

2 Heat 3 T. oil. Stir-fry **1** until meat changes color (Fig. 1), add **2** and stir-fry lightly(Fig. 2). Add **3** and bring to boil; add noodles. Lightly toss to mix (Fig. 3). Add vinegar and pepper as desired.

☐ **TO TENDERIZE MEAT:** Marinate in 1/2 T. each; soy sauce, cooking wine and cornstarch.

1 將乾麵條煮熟（同上）。

2 油3大匙燒熱，炒香 **1** 料至肉變色（圖1），隨入 **2** 料略炒（圖2），再加 **3** 料燒開，入麵條拌炒均勻即成（圖3）。可隨意加入醋、辣椒。

☐ **爲增加肉之滑嫩：** 可在肉絲內拌入醬油、酒、太白粉各$^1/_2$大匙再使用。

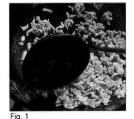
Fig. 1

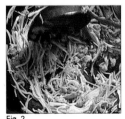
Fig. 2

Fig. 3

Tasty Meat Buns

包子

1 ¹/₃ lbs (600g) ground pork, beef, or chicken

2 T. soy sauce, 6 T. water
1 T. cooking wine
¹/₂ T. sesame oil, 1 t. sugar
dash of pepper

1 ¹/₂ T. cornstarch
3 T. chopped green onion
1 ¹/₂ T. chopped ginger root

1 ³/₄ c. warm water
¹/₄ c. sugar
¹/₂ T. powdered yeast

5 c. flour
2 T. oil or shortening

1 **FILLING:** Mix meat with **1** , then **2** ; mix thoroughly.

2 **DOUGH:** Put sugar of **3** in warm water and stir to dissolve. Sprinkle in yeast and let stand 10 minutes. The yeast will form a head and rise to top. Add flour and oil. Knead dough until smooth and elastic then cover with damp cloth. Let rise in a warm place 1-4 hours, or until doubled in bulk. Dough may also be placed in a warm oven for 1 hour to rise.

3 Knead dough on lightly floured surface until smooth and elastic. Roll dough into a long baton-like shape, then divide into 24 pieces. Roll each piece to form a thin circle, then place a portion of filling in each circle. Wrap dough to enclose filling (Fig. 1). Shape dough circle by pleating and pinching edges to form bun (Fig. 2, 3 & 4). Line steamer with damp cloth or small pieces of paper on which to set buns. Let buns stand 10 minutes then steam over high heat 12 minutes.

☐ Weather conditions may make flour damp, the quantity of water and flour when kneading must be adjusted to get a smooth, soft dough.

1 餡：絞肉先調 **1** 料，再加 **2** 料拌成肉餡。

2 皮：將 **3** 料的糖放進溫水內，待溶化後撒入酵母，擱置10分鐘上浮一層白沫，拌入麵粉及豬油揉搓成軟硬適中的麵糰，上蓋濕布，蓋1-4小時或麵糰發到二倍大（如放入烤箱保溫，則1小時即可）。

3 將發好麵塊揉搓至十分光滑，再揉成長條狀，分成24個小麵糰，再逐一擀壓成圓薄片；每張麵皮中央置1份餡，在皮邊上先掐一折（圖1），兩指合捏，再往前捏一折，再兩指合捏，如此反覆全部捏完成包子狀（圖2、3、4），底墊6公分四方之白紙或蒸籠內鋪上濕布擱置約10分鐘，再以大火蒸12分鐘即成。

☐ 麵粉因產地不同其乾度不一，故揉麵時太乾或太濕需酌量加水或麵粉。

絞肉（豬、牛或鷄）⋯⋯⋯⋯1斤
水⋯⋯⋯⋯⋯⋯⋯⋯⋯⋯⋯6大匙
醬油⋯⋯⋯⋯⋯⋯⋯⋯⋯⋯2大匙
酒⋯⋯⋯⋯⋯⋯⋯⋯⋯⋯⋯1大匙
麻油⋯⋯⋯⋯⋯⋯⋯⋯⋯¹/₂大匙
糖⋯⋯⋯⋯⋯⋯⋯⋯⋯⋯⋯1小匙
胡椒⋯⋯⋯⋯⋯⋯⋯⋯⋯⋯少許

太白粉⋯⋯⋯⋯⋯⋯⋯⋯1¹/₂大匙
蔥末⋯⋯⋯⋯⋯⋯⋯⋯⋯⋯3大匙
薑末⋯⋯⋯⋯⋯⋯⋯⋯⋯1¹/₂大匙

糖⋯⋯⋯⋯⋯⋯⋯⋯⋯⋯¹/₄杯
溫水⋯⋯⋯⋯⋯⋯⋯⋯⋯1³/₄杯
酵母⋯⋯⋯⋯⋯⋯⋯⋯⋯¹/₂大匙

麵粉⋯⋯⋯⋯⋯⋯⋯⋯⋯⋯5杯
豬油⋯⋯⋯⋯⋯⋯⋯⋯⋯⋯2大匙

Fig. 1

Fig. 2

Fig. 3

Fig. 4

Fried Won Tons

炸餛飩

1 Add **1** to meat. Mix thoroughly then divide into 30 portions.

2 Place one portion of mix in center of a won ton skin. Diagonally fold skin in half to form a triangle (Fig. 1); fold edge containing filling over about 1/2″ (1cm) (Fig. 2). Bring the two points together; moisten one inner edge and pinch the ends together to hold (Fig. 3).

3 Heat oil for deep-frying. Fry won tons over medium heat until golden. Maintain medium heat. If oil is too hot, meat will not cook and won ton skins may burn.

1 將絞肉調入 **1** 料拌勻，分成30份。

2 將餡置皮中間，折成三角形（圖1），由1公分處向前再折疊（圖2），由兩端沾水黏住（圖3）。

3 「炸油」燒熱，將餛飩炸至餡熟皮呈金黃色撈起。炸餛飩時油不要燒太熱，以免肉還未熟皮已焦黑。

$^1\!/_3$ **lb (150g) ground pork, beef or chicken**

1 $^1\!/_2$ T. water, 1 t. cornstarch
1 t. cooking wine, $^1\!/_2$ t. salt
pepper, sesame oil as desired

30 won ton skins
oil for deep-frying

絞肉（豬、牛或鷄）‥‥‥‥‥4兩

水‥‥‥‥‥‥‥‥‥‥‥1$\frac{1}{2}$大匙
太白粉、酒‥‥‥‥‥‥各1小匙
鹽‥‥‥‥‥‥‥‥‥‥$\frac{1}{2}$小匙
胡椒、麻油‥‥‥‥‥‥各少許

餛飩皮‥‥‥‥‥‥‥‥‥30張
「炸油」‥‥‥‥‥‥‥‥適量

Won Ton Soup

餛飩湯

1 Bring **1** to boil. Add won tons; bring to boil again and cook 4 more minutes. Add spinach and bring to boil. Add **2**; serve.

☐ **FOR CLEAR SOUP:** Cook won tons separately in another pot, then put in soup. Different brands of won ton skins have different thicknesses; select as desired.

1 將 **1** 料燒開，放入餛飩再燒開續煮4分鐘，加青菜燒開，再加 **2** 料即成。

☐ 若將餛飩在滾水內煮熟，再放入湯內其湯較清；餛飩皮有厚與薄，可依個人喜愛選用。

20 won tons

6 c. stock, 1 $^1\!/_4$ t. salt

$^1\!/_2$ **lb (225g) spinach**

1 t. sesame oil, 1 T. soy sauce
1 T. shredded ginger root or chopped green onions
dash of pepper

餛飩‥‥‥‥‥‥‥‥‥‥20個
高湯‥‥‥‥‥‥‥‥‥‥‥6杯
鹽‥‥‥‥‥‥‥‥‥‥1$\frac{1}{4}$小匙

青菜‥‥‥‥‥‥‥‥‥‥‥6兩

麻油‥‥‥‥‥‥‥‥‥‥1小匙
醬油‥‥‥‥‥‥‥‥‥‥1大匙
薑絲或蔥花‥‥‥‥‥‥1大匙
胡椒‥‥‥‥‥‥‥‥‥‥少許

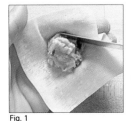

Fig. 1

Fig. 2

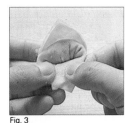

Fig. 3

Fried Egg Rolls

炸春捲

½ c. shredded pork, beef or chicken

1 t. cooking wine
1 t. cornstarch
¼ t. salt

4 c. shredded cabbage
total of 2 c. (shredded): celery, carrot

1 T. sugar
1 t. ea: salt, sesame oil
dash of pepper

16 egg roll skins

2 T. ea: flour, water

oil for deep-frying

1 Mix **1** with shredded meat. Heat 1 T. oil; stir-fry meat. Remove and set aside.

2 Blanch **2** in boiling water; remove and drain. Add meat and **3**; mix well (filling). Drain again when ready to use. Divide mixture into 16 portions.

3 Place a portion of filling in egg roll skin. Roll skin over filling to form a baton. Seal with mixture **4** (Figs. 1, 2, 3 & 4). Continue this process.

4 Heat oil for deep-frying. Fry egg rolls over medium heat 4 minutes, or until golden brown; remove and drain.

☐ Bean sprouts, yellow Chinese chives, bamboo shoots and string beans may be used for **2**.

☐ Most chinese markets sell egg roll skins. If frozen, allow to thaw to room temperature then separate each skin as it is used.

豬、牛或雞絲 ……………… ½杯

太白粉、酒 ……………… 各1小匙
鹽 ……………………… ¼小匙

高麗菜絲 ……………………… 4杯
芹菜絲、紅蘿蔔絲 ………… 共2杯

糖 ……………………………… 1大匙
鹽、麻油 ……………… 各1小匙
胡椒 ……………………… 少許

春捲皮 ……………………… 16張

麵粉、水 ……………… 各2大匙

「炸油」 ……………………… 適量

1 肉絲調入 **1** 料，油1大匙燒熱，將肉絲炒熟，備用。

2 將 **2** 料川燙瀝乾，與炒好的肉絲及 **3** 料拌勻成餡，分成16份，包時將汁瀝出。

3 春捲皮中間放餡，邊緣塗拌勻的 **4** 料，捲成圓筒狀（圖1、2、3、4）。

4 「炸油」燒熱，中火炸4分鐘至皮脆呈金黃色即成。

☐ 可任意選用 **2** 料內之材料，如綠豆芽、韭黃、筍、包心菜、四季豆等。

☐ 如購買冷凍春捲皮，等解凍後揭開即可使用。

Fig. 1

Fig. 2

Fig. 3

Fig. 4

Rice Pudding

八寶飯

1 c. dried fruits of preference
1 T. lard or butter
2 c. glutinous rice

3 T. sugar
2 T. lard or butter

¹/₂ c. red bean paste

1 c. water
3 T. sugar
2 t. cornstarch

1 Grease 7″ (16cm) heatproof bowl with 1 T. lard. Arrange dried fruit in circular fashion as shown (Fig. 1).

2 Cook rice as directed below. While rice is hot, mix with **1** ; place rice and red bean paste into greased bowl (Figs. 2, 3 & 4). Pack firmly. Steam over high heat 1 hour; remove. Place a serving dish on the bowl and invert to remove the rice.

3 Stir and bring **2** to boil, then pour over the rice pudding and serve.

☐ **TO PREPARE RED BEAN PASTE:** see p.91, or purchase paste from a Chinese market. If bean paste is not sweetened, add sugar to taste and mix.

☐ **TO COOK GLUTINOUS RICE:** Rinse 2 c. glutinous rice then soak in 1 1/2 cups water and let stand for 30 minutes, (glutinous rice requires less water than regular rice). Bring to boil over high heat. Allow to boil 1 minute; stir briefly. Cover and cook 20 minutes over low heat. Turn off heat, let stand 10 minutes with cover. Rice cooker may be used.

數種蜜餞 ·····················1杯
豬油 ·························1大匙
糯米 ··························2杯

豬油 ·························2大匙
糖 ·························3大匙

豆沙 ·························¹⁄₂杯

水 ·························1杯
糖 ·························3大匙
太白粉 ·····················2小匙

1 圓容器內擦抹豬油1大匙，將蜜餞排於容器底部（圖1）。

2 糯米洗淨，煮成飯，趁熱拌上 **1** 料。容器內填入飯及豆沙（圖2、3、4），大火蒸約60分鐘取出，倒扣盤內。

3 將 **2** 料攪拌燒開澆在八寶飯上即成。

☐ **豆沙做法**：見第91頁。

☐ **糯米飯煮法**：將2杯糯米洗淨瀝乾水，再加1½杯水浸泡30分鐘，用大火燒開煮1分鐘略攪，蓋鍋改小火續煮20分鐘，即熄火再燜10分鐘即可。亦可用電鍋煮成飯。煮糯米飯時，水的份量比一般米少。

Fig. 1

Fig. 2

Fig. 3

Fig. 4

Chinese Almond Jello

杏仁豆腐

1 ¼ oz. (7g) agar-agar (Fig. 1)
6 c. water

1 c. sugar

2 ³/₄ c. evaporated milk
1 T. almond extract

1 can of mixed fruit (8 ½ oz.)

1 洋菜（圖1）⋯⋯⋯⋯⋯⋯7公克
水⋯⋯⋯⋯⋯⋯⋯⋯⋯⋯⋯6杯

糖⋯⋯⋯⋯⋯⋯⋯⋯⋯⋯⋯1杯

2 濃縮奶水（1小罐）⋯⋯⋯⋯³⁄₄杯
杏仁精⋯⋯⋯⋯⋯⋯⋯⋯1大匙

水果罐（小）⋯⋯⋯⋯⋯⋯1罐

1 Mix **1** (Fig. 2) and let stand 30 minutes. Bring **1** to boil. Reduce heat to low and continue to cook until agar-agar dissolves. Add sugar and bring to boil. Add **2** (Fig. 3). Stir, then turn off heat. Pour into serving bowls (Fig. 4). Refrigerate until mixture sets. Add fruit before serving.

☐ The amount of agar-agar may be increased to set the jello harder. Dice jello and serve with fruit and crushed ice.

☐ Agar-agar may be purchased at most Chinese markets. If unavailable, use gelatin and follow directions on package.

1 將 **1** 料置30分鐘（圖2）後燒開，改小火煮至洋菜溶化時，加糖燒開，再加 **2** 料（圖3），攪勻熄火，倒入碗內（圖4），待涼凝固，可加水果食用。

☐ 參照上面做法，將洋菜份量略增加做成較硬的杏仁豆腐，切丁後可加入什錦水果丁，適量的糖水及碎冰一齊食用。

☐ 如無洋菜時可使用膠粉取代，並依照包裝上指示來做。

Fig. 1

Fig. 2

Fig. 3

Fig. 4

Shau Mai I

燒賣㈠

1 lb (450g) ground pork, beef or chicken

1

4 T. water
1 ¹/₂ T. soy sauce
1 ¹/₂ T. cornstarch
³/₄ T. cooking wine
¹/₂ t. sugar
³/₄ T. sesame oil
dash of pepper

2 c. flour

2

¹/₂ c. boiling water
dash of salt
¹/₄ c. cold water
1 T. oil or shortening

絞肉（豬、牛或鷄肉）……12兩

1

水 ……………………………4大匙
醬油、太白粉…………各1½大匙
酒、麻油 ……………各¾大匙
糖 ……………………………½小匙
胡椒 …………………………少許

麵粉 …………………………2杯

2

滾水 ……………………………½杯
鹽 ……………………………少許
冷水 ……………………………¼杯
豬油 …………………………1大匙

1 **FILLING:** Add **1** to meat; stir 5 minutes to mix thoroughly.

2 **DOUGH:** Add boiling water and salt of **2** to flour; mix. Add cold water and oil. Mix and knead smooth. Roll dough into long baton-like shape, then cut into 30 pieces. Use rolling pin to roll each portion into thin 2″ (6cm) circle. Ready-made won ton skins may be used in lieu of dough.

3 Place 1 portion of filling in middle of dough circle. Bring up opposite edges (Fig. 1) and pinch together to hold (Fig. 2). Shape loops (Fig. 3) for decoration. Loops may be filled with grated carrots, chopped black mushroom, cooked egg or green onion (Fig. 4). Line steamer with damp cloth or oil lightly. Set shau mai about 1 inch apart. Steam over high heat 5 minutes; remove and serve.

☐ Won ton skins may be folded in various ways.

1 餡：絞肉調 **1** 料攪拌5分鐘即成餡。

2 皮：麵粉加 **2** 料內的滾水和鹽攪拌，再入冷水及豬油揉成軟硬適中的麵糰；搓長條並分成30個小麵糰，再捍成直徑6公分薄皮。

3 將餡置皮中間（圖1），捏出四角洞（圖2、3），鑲入蛋、蔥葉、紅蘿蔔、香菇作裝飾（圖4），蒸籠內鋪濕布或塗油，上置燒賣大火蒸5分鐘即成。

☐ 燒賣形狀可隨意。

Fig. 1

Fig. 2

Fig. 3

Fig. 4

燒賣 (二)

1 ground pork, beef or chicken and diced shelled shrimp section:

1 lb (450g) ground pork, beef
 or chicken and diced shelled
 shrimp

1 ¹/₂ T. soy sauce
1 ¹/₂ T. cornstarch
³/₄ T. cooking wine
³/₄ T. sesame oil
¹/₂ t. sugar
dash of pepper
1 egg white

30 won ton skins

絞肉、蝦（切丁）	……… 共12兩
醬油、太白粉	……… 各1¹⁄₂大匙
酒、麻油	……… 各³⁄₄大匙
糖	……… ¹⁄₂小匙
胡椒	……… 少許
蛋白	……… 1個
餛飩皮	……… 30張

1 **FILLING:** Add **1** to meat and shrimp; stir 5 minutes to mix thoroughly.

2 **SKINS:** Cut off edges of won ton skins to form circles.

3 Place 1 portion of filling in center of won ton skin (Fig. 1). Gather won ton skin edges around filling. Dip a knife in water and use it to smooth meat surface (water will prevent meat from sticking to knife). Shau mai may be garnished by placing a green pea or shrimp on top (Figs. 2, 3 & 4). Line steamer with damp cloth or oil lightly. Steam over high heat 5 minutes; remove and serve.

☐ Won ton skins may be folded in various ways (see pictures on pp. 86 & 88). Ready-made won ton skins are available in Chinese markets. The thinner the skin, the better the result.

1 餡：絞肉及蝦調 **1** 料攪拌5分鐘即成餡。。

2 皮：餛飩皮修成圓形。

3 將餡置皮當中（圖1），捏成型，刀沾水在餡面上抹平，上置青豆或蝦作裝飾（圖2、3、4），蒸籠內鋪濕布或塗油，上置燒賣，大火蒸5分鐘即成。

☐ 燒賣形狀可隨意（見86、88頁），市面上售有現成餛飩皮。

Fig. 1

Fig. 2

Fig. 3

Fig. 4

Cantonese-Style Moon Cakes

廣式月餅

1 **FILLING:** Preheat oven to 350°F (178°C). Place egg yolks on cookie sheet and bake 15 minutes; remove. Divide bean paste into 20 portions. Put 1 egg yolk into 1 portion of bean paste; roll to enclose.

2 **DOUGH:** Beat **1** until sugar melts. Add **2** then **3**; lightly mix well. Divide into 20 portions.

3 Preheat oven to 400°F (205°C). Flatten each dough portion to 4" (10cm) circle. Place 1 portion of filling in center of circle and wrap to enclose. Lightly flour mold and place filled dough into mold (Fig. 1); press dough to fill mold. Gently tap to release (Fig. 2). Place on cookie sheet and brush egg yolk over dough. Bake on middle rack 30 minutes or until golden.

METHOD FOR MAKING RED BEAN PASTE:

☐ Rinse and soak beans in water overnight (or, immerse in cold water, bring to boil, turn off heat and soak for 1 hour). Drain and discard water. Add 7 cups of water to the beans; cover and bring to boil. Reduce heat to medium and cook 1 1/2 hours until beans soften.

☐ Stir the beans continuosly over high heat until liquid has almost evaporated. Add **4**, stir continuously for 10-15 minutes (makes 4 lbs. {1350g} of bean paste). After refrigerating, bean paste consistency should be thick enough to make into balls. (See p. 83, Fig. 3).

---

20 salty egg yolks
2 ²/₃ lbs (1200g) red bean
  paste

3 eggs , 1 ¼ c. sugar

³/₄ c. melted butter, ½ t. salt

4 c. flour, 1 T. baking powder
½ c. powdered milk

1 egg yolk
1 mold

1 ¹/₃ lbs (600g) red beans

2 c. sugar
³/₄ c. oil or shortening

鹹蛋黃 ⋯⋯⋯⋯⋯⋯⋯⋯20個
豆沙⋯⋯⋯⋯⋯⋯⋯⋯⋯2斤

糖⋯⋯⋯⋯⋯⋯⋯⋯⋯1¼杯
蛋⋯⋯⋯⋯⋯⋯⋯⋯⋯⋯3個

奶油（溶化）⋯⋯⋯⋯¾杯
鹽⋯⋯⋯⋯⋯⋯⋯⋯⋯½小匙

麵粉⋯⋯⋯⋯⋯⋯⋯⋯4杯
奶粉⋯⋯⋯⋯⋯⋯⋯⋯½杯
發粉⋯⋯⋯⋯⋯⋯⋯⋯1大匙

蛋黃⋯⋯⋯⋯⋯⋯⋯⋯1個
月餅模型⋯⋯⋯⋯⋯⋯1個

紅豆⋯⋯⋯⋯⋯⋯⋯⋯1斤

糖⋯⋯⋯⋯⋯⋯⋯⋯⋯2杯
豬油或植物性白油 ⋯⋯⋯¾杯

---

1 餡：鹹蛋黃置於烤盤內，以350℉烤15分鐘。豆沙分成20份，逐一將蛋黃包成圓球狀。

2 皮：把 **1** 料攪至糖溶化，拌入 **2** 料，再加 **3** 料輕拌勻，分成20塊小麵糰。

3 模型內撒入少許麵粉，將小麵糰壓成直徑10公分圓形麵皮，把豆沙球包好，裝入模型內（圖1）壓緊，印好花樣輕扣倒出（圖2），置烤盤，上面塗蛋黃，將烤箱燒熱至400℉，放中層烤30分鐘至金黃色即成。

豆沙做法：

☐ 紅豆泡水一夜（或將紅豆泡在滾水內1小時），待豆膨脹，倒出水再重新加水7杯燒開，改中火蓋鍋90分鐘至紅豆裂開。

☐ 將煮好的紅豆開大火邊煮邊攪把水份蒸發至略收乾，加 **4** 料（變稀）繼續用大火邊煮邊攪約10-15分鐘，可做豆沙3斤。做好的豆沙需軟硬適中，冰涼後才能搓圓（見83頁圖3）。

Fig. 1

Fig. 2

1 ⅓ lbs (600g) red bean paste
(see p. 91)

(see p. 91)

1 2 c. flour, ⅔ c. water
4 T. shortening or butter
½ T. sugar, ⅓ t. salt

2 1 c. flour, 5 T. oil or shortening

damp towel or cloth
red food coloring
stamp design of choice

½ c. lard, shortening or butter
¾ c. sugar

1 1 T. water, ½ t. baking soda
1 t. baking powder

2 1 egg, ½ t. almond extract

2 c. flour
24 whole almonds, peanuts
or sesame seeds

Fig. 1

Fig. 2

Fig. 3

Short Moon Cakes

蘇式月餅

豆沙（做法見91頁）⋯⋯⋯1斤

麵粉⋯⋯⋯⋯⋯⋯⋯⋯⋯2杯
水⋯⋯⋯⋯⋯⋯⋯⋯⋯⋯$\frac{2}{3}$杯
豬油或奶油⋯⋯⋯⋯⋯⋯4大匙
糖⋯⋯⋯⋯⋯⋯⋯⋯⋯$\frac{1}{2}$大匙
鹽⋯⋯⋯⋯⋯⋯⋯⋯⋯$\frac{1}{3}$小匙

麵粉⋯⋯⋯⋯⋯⋯⋯⋯⋯1杯
豬油⋯⋯⋯⋯⋯⋯⋯⋯⋯5大匙

食用紅色水⋯⋯⋯⋯⋯⋯適量
紙巾⋯⋯⋯⋯⋯⋯⋯⋯⋯1小張

印花模型⋯⋯⋯⋯⋯⋯⋯1個

1 **FILLING:** Divide bean paste into 20 portions and shape into balls. Dough A: Mix **1**; make dough and knead until smooth. Divide into 20 pieces. Dough B: Repeat same procedure with mixture **2**.

2 Flatten pieces of dough A to circles. Put a piece of dough B in the center of dough A (Fig. 1); flatten lightly with palm of hand. Use rolling pin to roll each piece into a rectangle. Roll each piece into baton-like shape (Fig. 2). Place dough vertically then roll out again to a rectangle. Roll dough into baton-like shape. Lightly flatten a portion of dough with palm of hand, using rolling pin to form 3″ (8 cm) circle. Place filling in center; gather edges of dough to completely enclose. Place on cookie sheet.

3 Add a few drops of food coloring to damp towel. Press stamp design on towel, then lightly stamp dough (Fig. 3) or brush 1 egg on dough (P.93, bottom). Place cakes on cookie sheet; bake cakes 25 minutes on middle rack at 350°F (178°C) in preheated oven. Remove and serve.

1 餡：豆沙分揉成20個圓球。將 **1** 料及 **2** 料分別拌合成麵糰，即爲「水油皮」與「油心」，也各分成20個小麵糰。

2 「水油皮」包「油心」（圖1）壓扁擀長由邊捲成筒狀（圖2），放直再擀長，再捲成筒狀，用手略壓擀成直徑8公分之圓形，將豆沙球包好置烤盤。

3 印花模型沾 **3** 料（紙巾先沾水，擠乾，再加紅色水），在圓餅上加蓋花樣（圖3）或塗打散之蛋液（左頁下圖）；烤箱燒熱至350℉，放中層烤25分鐘至膨起即可。

Chinese Almond Cookies

杏仁酥

奶油或豬油⋯⋯⋯⋯⋯⋯$\frac{1}{2}$杯
糖⋯⋯⋯⋯⋯⋯⋯⋯⋯$\frac{3}{4}$杯

水⋯⋯⋯⋯⋯⋯⋯⋯⋯⋯1大匙
小蘇打⋯⋯⋯⋯⋯⋯⋯$\frac{1}{2}$小匙
發粉⋯⋯⋯⋯⋯⋯⋯⋯⋯1小匙

杏仁精⋯⋯⋯⋯⋯⋯⋯$\frac{1}{2}$小匙
蛋⋯⋯⋯⋯⋯⋯⋯⋯⋯⋯1個

麵粉⋯⋯⋯⋯⋯⋯⋯⋯⋯2杯
杏仁（花生或芝麻）⋯⋯24粒

1 Preheat oven to 350°F (178°C). Melt butter then add sugar and beat. Add mixtures **1** and **2**; beat 2 minutes. Add flour and mix to form dough.

2 Divide dough into 24 balls and place on greased cookie sheet. Place almond in center of each ball then lightly flatten. Bake on lower rack of oven 15 minutes; remove when golden. Serve.

1 奶油先溶化，加糖用打蛋器攪拌，再加拌好的 **1** 料及 **2** 料攪拌約2分鐘，隨入麵粉輕拌成軟硬適中的麵糰。

2 做好的麵糰搓成長條，再切24小塊，每塊揉成圓球形，中央置杏仁，輕壓成餅狀；烤箱燒熱至350℉，置下層烤約15分鐘呈金黃色即成。

INDEX

索引

WEI-CHUAN COOKBOOKS

CHINESE CUISINE
CHINESE COOKING MADE EASY
CHINESE CUISINE
CHINESE COOKING FAVORITE HOME DISHES
CHINESE COOKING FOR BEGINNERS [1]
CHINESE RICE & NOODLES
RICE, CHINESE HOME-COOKING
FISH, CHINESE STYLE MADE EASY [2]
SHELLFISH, CHINESE STYLE MADE EASY [2]

CHINESE REGIONAL CUISINE
CHINESE CUISINE, BEIJING STYLE
CHINESE CUISINE, CANTONESE STYLE
CHINESE CUISINE, SHANGHAI STYLE

CHINESE CUISINE, SZECHWAN STYLE
CHINESE CUISINE, TAIWANESE STYLE

GARNISHES
CHINESE GARNISHES [3]
GREAT GARNISHES

HEALTHFUL COOKING
CHINESE HERB COOKING FOR HEALTH
CHINESE HOME COOKING FOR HEALTH
LOW-CHOLESTEROL CHINESE CUISINE
SIMPLY VEGETARIAN
VEGETARIAN COOKING

INTERNATIONAL CUISINE
INDIAN CUISINE
JAPANESE CUISINE [4]
KOREAN CUISINE
MEXICAN COOKING MADE EASY [5]
ONE DISH MEALS FROM POPULAR CUISINES [2]
SINGAPOREAN, MALAYSIAN, & INDONESIAN CUISINE
THAI COOKING MADE EASY [6]
VIETNAMESE CUISINE

SPECIALTIES
CHINESE DIM SUM
CHINESE SNACKS, REVISED
CREATIVE CHINESE OVEN COOKING

COMPACT COOKBOOK SERIES
SOUP! SOUP! SOUP!
TOFU! TOFU! TOFU!
VERY! VERY! VEGETARIAN!

VIDEOS
CHINESE GARNISHES I [8]
CHINESE GARNISHES II [8]

• ALL COOKBOOKS ARE BILINGUAL (ENGLISH/CHINESE) UNLESS FOOTNOTED OTHERWISE •

1. Also available in English/Spanish, French/Chinese, and German/Chinese   **2**. Trilingual English/Chinese/Spanish edition
3. Bilingual English/Spanish Only   **4**. Also available in Chinese/French   **5**. Also available in English/Spanish
6. Also available in English/French   **7**. English and Chinese are in separate editions   **8**. English Only

---

味全叢書

中國菜系列
中國菜
速簡中國菜
實用中國菜 [1]
實用家庭菜
魚 [2]
蝦、貝、蟹 [2]

省份菜
上海菜
四川菜
北京菜
台灣菜
廣東菜

拼盤·米·麵
盤飾精選
米麵簡餐
米食，家常篇

健康系列
養生藥膳
養生家常菜
均衡飲食
健康素
素食

點心·烘焙·燒烤
點心專輯
飲茶食譜
創意燒烤

異國風味
南洋菜
泰國菜 [4]
越南菜
印度菜
韓國菜
日本料理 [5]
墨西哥菜 [3]
簡餐（五國風味）[2]

小食譜
豆腐
湯
家庭素食
牛肉 [6]
雞肉 [6]
蔬菜 [6]

（如無數字標註，即為中英對照版）

1. 中英、英西、中法、中德版   **2**. 中英西對照版   **3**. 中英版及英西版   **4**. 中英版及中法版   **5**. 中英版及中法版   **6**. 中文版及英文版

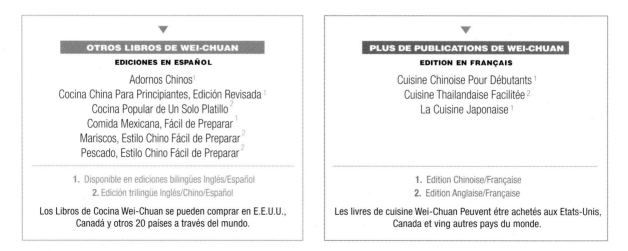

OTROS LIBROS DE WEI-CHUAN
EDICIONES EN ESPAÑOL

Adornos Chinos [1]
Cocina China Para Principiantes, Edición Revisada [1]
Cocina Popular de Un Solo Platillo [2]
Comida Mexicana, Fácil de Preparar [1]
Mariscos, Estilo Chino Fácil de Preparar [2]
Pescado, Estilo Chino Fácil de Preparar [2]

1. Disponible en ediciones bilingües Inglés/Español
2. Edición trilingüe Inglés/Chino/Español

Los Libros de Cocina Wei-Chuan se pueden comprar en E.E.U.U.,
Canadá y otros 20 países a través del mundo.

PLUS DE PUBLICATIONS DE WEI-CHUAN
EDITION EN FRANÇAIS

Cuisine Chinoise Pour Débutants [1]
Cuisine Thailandaise Facilitée [2]
La Cuisine Japonaise [1]

1. Edition Chinoise/Française
2. Edition Anglaise/Française

Les livres de cuisine Wei-Chuan Peuvent être achetés aux Etats-Unis,
Canada et ving autres pays du monde.

Wei-Chuan Cookbooks can be purchased in the U.S.A., Canada and twenty other countries worldwide
1455 Monterey Pass Road, #110, Monterey Park, CA 91754, U.S.A. • Tel: (323)261-3880 • Fax: (323) 261-3299
E-Mail: wc@weichuancookbook.com • Website: www.weichuancookbook.com